M000249106

FAST BREAK TO LINE BREAK

ALSO BY TODD DAVIS

FAST BREAK
TO LINE BREAK

Poets on the Art of Basketball

Edited by Todd Davis

Michigan State University Press

East Lansing

Copyright © 2012 by Michigan State University

⊛ The paper used in this publication meets the minimum requirements of ANSI/NISO
Z39.48-1992 (R 1997) (Permanence of Paper).

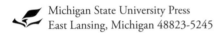 Michigan State University Press
East Lansing, Michigan 48823-5245

Printed and bound in the United States of America.

18 17 16 15 14 13 12   1 2 3 4 5 6 7 8 9 10

LIBRARY OF CONGRESS CATALOGING-IN-PUBLICATION DATA

Fast break to line break : poets on the art of basketball / edited by Todd Davis.
    p. cm.
    ISBN 978-1-61186-035-1 (pbk. : alk. paper) 1. Basketball. 2. Sports—Poetry. I. Davis,
Todd.
GV885.F37 2012
796.323—dc23
2011024668

Cover design by Erin Kirk New

Book design by Scribe Inc. (www.scribenet.com)

Cover photograph is by Dinty W. Moore and is used with permission.

green
press
INITIATIVE Michigan State University Press is a member of the Green Press Initiative and
is committed to developing and encouraging ecologically responsible publishing
practices. For more information about the Green Press Initiative and the use of recycled
paper in book publishing, please visit www.greenpressinitiative.org.

Visit Michigan State University Press on the World Wide Web at:
www.msupress.msu.edu

For my favorite players—
Shelly, Noah, and Nathan

THE GAME

FOURTH QUARTER

OVERTIME

PREGAME

BASKETBALL, POETRY, AND

ALL THINGS BEAUTIFUL

TODD DAVIS AND J. D. SCRIMGEOUR

In December 1891, just three months before the death of Walt Whitman, Dr. James Naismith nailed two peach baskets to the wall of the gymnasium at the YMCA International Training School in Springfield, Massachusetts. Taking up the challenge of his department chair to create some indoor recreation for the winter months, Naismith considered the formal rules of American sport and improvised. He built his game out of the materials at hand: a pastiche of conventions garnered from sports as diverse as rugby and lacrosse and punctuated with a discarded soccer ball and the peach baskets that the janitor found in a storeroom.

Whitman doubtless would have been pleased with Naismith's game, born of necessity and joy, requiring ego and egolessness. A game with patterns that can feel elemental, yet distinguished by improbable improvisations, full of the energy of the city and the stillness (ever taken a foul shot?) of the prairie—an American game. Indeed, one might imagine Whitman's spirit transferring from his body into this new game and the bodies that play

3

it, their moves graceful as grasses in the wind, stunning as sunlight flashing off the East River.

As kids we knew immediately what poetry was when we saw Julius Erving float toward the basket, ball scooped in his large hand, every bodily signal suggesting that this athlete would either lay it in on the right side or flush it with a flourishing dunk, only to see that free verse is simply a riff on formal intention as the good Doctor defied gravity and flew to the other side of the basket where, with a windmilling hook, he scored on a reverse.

Likewise, what baller wouldn't recognize the dramatic tension—epic verse as startling as any battle Odysseus fought—as Willis Reed gingerly stepped onto Madison Square Garden's floor, body ragged and wracked, to deliver turnaround jump shot after turnaround jump shot with a soft touch of lyricism and the triumphant joy of mortal victory.

Like the origins of the poetry that Whitman embraced and imagined— communal, oral, and mythmaking—basketball has been a game that many neighborhoods have come to revolve around. This is the place where trash-talking is elevated to poetic heights and where myths are made by girls who drain jumpers from five feet behind the three-point arc. This is the home so many of us long for where legendary boys leap high enough to make change from the mythical dollar we've been told rests at the top of all playground backboards. This is the liminal space where art and body are fused, where poetry is imagined and reimagined within the beauty of an orange sphere.

If baseball is the sport of elegant prose, basketball may be the sport of verse. From line break to fast break, from leaps of thought to the rising of the poetic body on the page, many poets have been drawn to basketball and its remarkable qualities. One poet actually watched and taped and then rewatched every game Larry Bird played in college and the pros. Another used Connie Hawkins's own tragic story to talk to her students about the tools a poet needs most: love and perseverance. There's even a poet who teaches students to take risks in their own work by introducing them to the moves of such scoring dervishes as LeBron James and Kobe Bryant.

In our travels to give readings we've come to know many poets who still lace up the shoes, who still treasure the trajectory of a long three or a threaded pass as much as they do the concluding line of a poem that shifts toward a fitting end. What a joy to see that our art brings us into the bonds of basketball, that when we talk about Nash, we may mean a poet or a point guard, that Jordan may be Michael or June. How much better we are to have heard Quincy Troupe immortalize Magic Johnson in lines as daring and unexpected as a six-foot, nine-inch point guard with a secret sky-hook: "Take the sucker to the hoop, 'magic' Johnson / recreate reverse hoodoo gems off the spin / deal alley-oop-dunk-a-thon-magician passes, now / double-pump, scissor, vamp through space, hang in place / & put it all in the sucker's face." This is the joy of poetry and basketball, the artistic and physical beauty of the game, which can never be parsed.

But what difference has this love, this joy of sport made in the creation of our poems and our lives as writers? In this collection of essays, poets meditate on what the game has meant to them personally, upon its impact on their art, upon the intersections of the body and writing about the body, about how a ball and a metal rim somehow have affected their lives and their lines, the sounds that connect them to others, poetic teammates all, in the same way the artistry of a well-thrown pass leads to a score or a juke-drive leaves us with jaws open in wonder.

FIRST QUARTER

HIDDEN TALENTS FAIL

TO MATERIALIZE

JIM DANIELS

SOME POETS TALK ABOUT BASEBALL AS THE MOST POETIC OF SPORTS because there is no clock, but I think sometimes poetry needs a clock—that sense of urgency created by the seconds ticking down. For my money, basketball is the most poetic of the major sports. The problem is that my money doesn't go very far, because when I played JV basketball at Fitzgerald High School, the only point I scored the whole season was a free throw after time had expired.

Basketball is also the most visibly sweaty of all major sports. The hot gym, the confined space, the towels to mop up sweat when the bodies fall to the hardwood. I've always liked my poetry with a little sweat in it. Though again I contradict myself, for I worked up very little sweat as the twelfth man on a thirteen-man team. The JV coach, Mr. Barkley, the chemistry teacher and backfield coach for the varsity football team, only put me in for the last minute or so. Sometimes just the last thirty seconds. No matter how badly we were losing. And every game was a loss.

You can learn a lot sitting on the bench—another bit of conventional wisdom—but I'm afraid I learned nothing (about basketball, at least). I spent a lot of time admiring the cheerleaders. Unlike basketball, poetry is not a team sport. That same year, I began writing poetry.

After tryouts had ended and the final roster was posted, I walked home with my friend Ron, who had been cut. Ron and I often played driveway hoops in the neighborhood. Tim, who was in my older brother Dave's class, called him Fat Ron, but he was never obese, and actually had slimmed down a lot by high school. But no one ever called him *Fast* Ron. He was my best friend, and it was a long walk home. He was passive and polite, even when drunk or stoned, so he wasn't visibly angry about not making the team; he was silent. I was silent. Silence—I was beginning to notice how one silence was different than another.

Two years later, Ron's father died in a car accident. Ron had been in the car and had gotten some cuts on his face, but otherwise was okay. Ron and I had always walked to school together. He lived a little farther away, so I'd wait for him to come down the street, then joined him. The morning after his father died, I assumed I would be walking to school alone, but as I stepped out the door, I spotted him, head down, coming toward me. Apparently, his mother was a wreck, and he didn't know what else to do, so he'd gotten himself up and got ready for school like any other day. I stood on the sidewalk waiting, trying to think of what I could possibly say to him. When he reached me, I got in step with him. We didn't say a word. A silence that dwarfed being cut from a basketball team.

When we got to school and were waiting for the bell to ring, somebody gave him a hard time about his scratched-up face, and I said, "Leave him alone, his dad just died."

So, there I was at the free-throw line, fouled at the buzzer while attempting one of my patented desperation shots—all my shots were desperation shots. Despite the game being over—another lopsided loss—the referee made sure I got my two free throws. The stands were filled for the varsity game coming up next. The varsity guys stood on the edge of the court, restless to start warming up. But I was going to get my shots.

The only reason I made the team, I think, was because Coach Barkley thought I had some of my brother Dave's athletic skills buried in me somewhere—hidden potential. Dave was captain of the football team, star running back, all conference, all county. I think he averaged over nine yards a carry his senior year. He was a National Merit Scholar. Harvard wanted to meet with him, but my parents said they couldn't afford Harvard. They were naïve in the ways of colleges, and didn't understand financial aid.

When Dave got a full ride to Michigan Tech by winning a scholarship funded by a local engineering firm, my parents were thrilled. It was a big deal that he was simply going to college, and the fact that he was going away from home to go to college carried with it a certain prestige. Going to college out of state was unheard of in our community.

My oldest brother Mike had gone to the community college—Twelve Mile High, we called it, because it was on Twelve Mile Road—one semester, then got a job at a truck repair place across the street from the Chrysler plant, where he would later work as a truck driver.

I was the number three son, and the jury was out as to just what I was going to end up doing. I hadn't been tracked college prep, and it wasn't until my junior year that I worked my way into those courses, motivated by the knowledge that in order to be a writer, I had to go to college. That year, I was in Earth Science, a class for those *not* going to college. I'd been relegated to that group in my move over from the Catholic school. It could've been those Cs and Ds in Conduct and Effort and Study Habits, along with all the checkmarks for bad behavior. In eighth grade, I had started to question all of the elements of faith that had been drilled into me by the nuns. That questioning, that not accepting what others told me, was another element that led me to poetry. In poetry, it seemed, you couldn't get into trouble by asking too many questions. You were supposed to ask questions. I turned out not to be a team player for the faith, though at that age I wasn't mature enough to figure out how to express my doubts without being a jerk about it.

Being a jerk had helped put me in Earth Science. The smart kids were taking Biology, then Chemistry, then Physics.

I think we all have those moments in our lives where we're swinging by the hinges and can go either way. A lot of those moments come when we're too young to recognize them, too full of ourselves to see beyond the present. We need a little luck sometimes to swing the right way.

If you played on varsity, the cheerleaders made a poster for you and put it on your school locker on every game day. They were supposed to make locker posters for the JV team for one game that season, but for some reason, I didn't get one. I remember my disappointment at not getting that kind of recognition, even just for that one time. I didn't want to admit it to myself. I wanted to be too cool to care, but I cared. I wanted some cheerleader spelling out the letters of my name.

My brother's crew of bulky football players sat in the section of bleachers nearest the cheerleaders. They all wore their letter jackets. Sitting on the bench, I'd seen them enter together as our game wound down. Everywhere they went, they made an entrance. If my brother had not been one of them, I probably would have hated them.

Brother Mike had been allied with the greaser contingent. While he was not a particularly tough guy, nobody messed with him or his crowd. They worked on their cars a lot. Drank a lot. I don't think any of them went to college. I'm not sure they all even finished high school. I had Mike on the one side, and Dave on the other. I was not a jock. I was not a tough guy. And if I was a poet, I sure as hell wasn't going to be telling anyone. That would elicit scorn from all sides. No locker posters for poets.

In the parking lot in front of Bur-Ler's, a five-and-dime across the street from the school, Ed Tarkowski had jumped on me. I do not remember the circumstances leading up to that, but I remember lying in the crumbling blacktop of the parking lot with Tarkowski on top of me and thinking that I very well might be in the process of getting my ass kicked. A crowd had gathered, and someone shouted something like "C'mon, Daniels." Then, out of nowhere a big tough guy I had never seen before pulled Tarkowski off of me. He asked, "Are you a Daniels?" I said yes. He asked, "Do you want to fight this guy?" I said no. He kicked Tarkowski in the ass and said, "Get the hell out of here." He was obviously a friend of my brother Mike's. I hold that public moment up next to my one point, two moments where being a Daniels had paid off.

Having two brothers kept me from walling myself off from other groups at the school. It helped me see the human side of people who were not like me. It made me a better poet.

I tossed up my first free throw. It was not a pretty shot. I had no pretty shots. It bounced off the rim a couple of times before dropping in. My brother and his friends went wild. I turned back to where they were sitting, startled. I broke into a big smile. I didn't think anyone had been paying attention, and I suspect if it weren't for my brother, they wouldn't have been.

I once accumulated three fouls in my minute and a half. Coach Barkley just shook his head. He had this expressive face that featured a menacing grimace that suggested excruciating pain. I became very familiar with that face. But when I got in the game, I had nothing to lose. I went crazy out there, tossing up wild shots, hacking everybody. It was kind of like eighth grade in Catholic school all over again.

Once, I told the coach to put the thirteenth man, Nick, in ahead of me. After I scored my one point, that put me ahead of Nick, and Nick played football and baseball, so he had more at stake. That big zero next to his name was something that he'd have to live with for two more years, or maybe the rest of his life.

Here's an excerpt from "No Relation," a prose poem I wrote about Nick:

> I quit scouts after six months to pursue my basketball career unimpeded.
> My last year I scored one point for an 0–16 team. One point the whole
> fucking season. I tried to write that without using fuck. Nick Manfred,
> who scored zero points, was killed by a drunk driver in California. I

13

couldn't make that up, about the one point. I lied about Nick—he lived in a vegetative state for years before actually dying. Basketball was his worst sport. He was a center in football, a catcher in baseball. His jockstrap was always yanked halfway up his back. He'd go in for the last thirty seconds and toss up shots from half-court that bounced off the rafters. Everyone thought that was funny except me and Nick. My one point killed him.

1972, that's what I've left out.

1972: The varsity coach/athletic director, Mr. Dick Simpson, was just called "the Dick" by most of the athletes. And many of the best athletes did not play sports at all. Simpson had a flattop haircut that resembled a perfectly tended lawn, the kind of lawn our fathers dreamt about as an antidote to the dark, dirty, factory they worked in.

1972: The drinking age was eighteen, which meant, with trickle down, my friends and I had started drinking in ninth grade.

1972: Nearly everybody had long hair, even the tough guys, though there were only two identifiable hippies in our school of twelve hundred. Jim Tarpinski and Mike Clancy. Tarpinski may also have been the tallest kid in the school. He was identifiable as a hippie because Donald Litinger, our local right-wing fanatic, had attacked him at some rally because he was wearing an American flag T-shirt, and that offended Mr. Litinger, who had an uncanny resemblance to Lee Harvey Oswald and could very well have shot Tarpinski. Tarpinski wandered the halls, a head above everyone else, his long frizzy hair making him seem even taller. He was an easy target for what was wrong with our society and our basketball team.

1972: To play basketball at our school, you had to have short hair like Mr. Simpson. As a result, many of the free-form artists of the court refused to play. Nevertheless, they attended the games. Ken Salvador had played in ninth grade, but then refused to cut his hair in tenth. He'd sit in the bleachers, stoned out of his mind, watching the games and laughing at inappropriate moments.

Mike Clancy was my friend. He sat in front of me in Earth Science. He did the daily school announcements, which meant he got to choose the music that played in the hallways while we changed classes. Occasionally, he let me make requests. Once I gave him my Woodstock album and asked him to play "Soul Sacrifice" by Santana. What a great song to change classes to. I recommend it highly.

I'm glad I started out in classes like Earth Science so that I could make friends with people like Mike Clancy, one of the gentlest guys in the school. He may have ended up being gay—no one at our high school ever dared to come out.

The thing about poetry is that everything is related. There's no such thing as "No Relation." So, when I write about poetry and basketball, I'm saying that everything's related, even though sometimes it seems like nothing's related.

My point is this:

The Friday of Thanksgiving week, Ron's parents were out somewhere, and he asked me to come over and drink from his parents' well-stocked bar, which we had taken to doing on occasion. In the middle of getting drunk, I remembered I had basketball practice that day and rushed over to the gym.

I practiced drunk, and no one seemed to notice. I wish now that somebody had. Later that season, Kevin Rogers, who was on the team, came to a game drunk and threw up in the locker room during warm-ups.

Kevin later borrowed his brother's car and had an accident that killed Jeff Zelinsk, who was class president at the time. They were drunk.

I showed up drunk at the next high school dance, and one of the cheerleaders confronted me, saying that, after what happened, how could I?

Luck. Stupidity. Luck. Stupidity.

Our senior year, Ron and I coached a Little League basketball team together. Our team won the championship, and I still have the trophy, though the plate that says "Head Coach: Jim Daniels" fell off.

How did two lousy players like us coach a bunch of fifth- and sixth-graders to a championship? Maybe I lied. Maybe I learned a few things about sitting on a bench while sitting on the bench. I don't remember a lot about that season, except that we made sure everyone scored by the end of the year.

Improvisation out of a set play.

HIDDEN TALENTS FAIL TO MATERIALIZE was the yearbook headline for my basketball team. That headline seems vaguely oxymoronic as I look at it now. But it also seems right when I think about both my basketball career and poetry. The coach assumed I had some hidden talent that might emerge over time. He was wrong. But I was beginning to think about hidden things a lot that year, about what went unsaid, about what was happening beneath the surface of my daily life. I never played on a school team again. As soon as the basketball season ended, I got a job in a local party store, a job I kept for two and a half years. Playing basketball had allowed me to get out of gym class, which in our school tended to resemble *Lord of the Flies,* featuring naked swimming and naked brutality, bullying of the first degree.

Dave and I have never talked about my one point. We were never explicit about how we felt about each other back in those days. It only happened through indirection, the smoke and mirrors of the teenage years.

Okay, I think I've got it now. Give me the ball.

When the football team stood and cheered after my one free throw, I'd had a moment that no one else on that team had the entire season. You can say what you want about their cheers being half-mocking, but I prefer to think that the emotional transference that happens in any good poem was happening then, that those guys, and the others who joined them in cheering, were perhaps thinking about what they might be feeling if they were in my place, getting the spotlight after a season in the shadows. Perhaps thinking of all the things that they were not good at. Sharing in my triumphant moment, however brief. The coaches and the other players were already headed toward the locker room, or were in the locker room already, but I had my audience, and we'd made a connection as satisfying as any success-ful poem.

My heart swelled as I stood there waiting for the referee to hand me the ball for my second shot, which, of course, I missed. Missing that second shot made the first one mean that much more.

BASKETBALL AND POETRY

The Two Richies

STEPHEN DUNN

BASKETBALL WAS MY FIRST LOVE. OR PERHAPS IT WAS MY RELIGION, if religion can be defined as that which most governs your life. As a teenager, I played almost every day, sometimes shoveling snow off the schoolyard court in order to do so. Sometimes I played in the dark, a distant streetlight the only illumination. If there was no one to play with I played by myself, imagining opponents or just practicing my shots. By the time I was fourteen I was five feet eleven, and the only freshman to make the varsity high school team. But I remember the coach looking at my small feet and shaking his head. "You're not going to get any bigger," he said, and he was right. I set about cultivating skills appropriate to someone my size. Shooting. Ball-handling. And I *thought* basketball when I wasn't playing it.

Since my midtwenties, I've written and thought poetry that way, a lover's way, at odd hours, my whole self, or as much of myself as I could bring to the task, involved. "Play for mortal stakes," Robert Frost called it. And often it is a kind of serious play, play that brings one closer to self and reality, and thus is not always pleasurable. Basketball, on the other hand, served to delay my entry into the real world, which of course was part of why I loved it.

I think that if it hadn't been for Richie Swartz and Butch van Breda Kolff's decision to play him instead of me as the shooting guard on the 1960 Hofstra College basketball team, I might have been able to delay such entry indefinitely. But after a good sophomore year in which I was the team's second highest scorer, Richie Swartz showed up and began for me a two-year lesson, often humiliating, about limits. Richie Swartz was good, pure and simple. But basketball is a game of relativities; the correct word is "better." Swartz was better than I. From the first time we covered each other in practice this was evident. He could block my jump shot. He could steal the ball from me. The writing, as they say, was on the wall, and it wasn't poetry.

If basketball offers you the possibility of transcendence, it more regularly offers you a sense of your limitations, though the two are sometimes intertwined. Every opponent presents to you a different set of latitudes or confinements. But basketball is a team game, and a good coach and good teammates can make use of your limitations, even free you from annoying defenders. No one could free me from Richie Swartz. Richie Swartz turned me inward to where doubts are, and doubts, while good for the poet, are bad for the athlete. In retrospect, Swartz turned me further toward the examined life, which, as everyone knows, is where angst resides. I accepted it as fully as I did the existential literature I was reading at the time. It's only the fool who denies that his jump shot has been cleanly blocked, or that he's suddenly empty handed. You are what you do, and don't do. Worse, it was all so public. I didn't have any face-saving lies to tell. No, I had plenty. All transparent.

In basketball it's common to play with people better than you. To grow up on the schoolyards in Queens was to know something about hierarchy and pecking orders. I had sought out good players because they were the yardsticks by which I could measure and sometimes exceed myself. But I had never before had to play every day against someone who so consistently prevented me from being effective, and that ineffectiveness carried over into game situations. Hesitant that entire year, 1960, I rarely played as well as I had the year before.

The equivalent in poetry writing would be not just to know, say, that

Yeats is a great poet (obviously that's desirable), but to have the achievements of Yeats block your ability to write poetry every time you tried. The poets who keep writing do so in the face of such greatness; if they were reasonable, they'd stop. There's much to be said for obsessiveness and stubbornness. Poets need to be somewhat driven in order to push forward; talent isn't quite enough.

I didn't let Richie Swartz entirely defeat me. I just made some adjustments with how to live with my first love. There's always a Richie Swartz out there, antithesis to your thesis. As the poet Robert Haas wrote in an epigraph to his book *Praise*, "We asked the captain what course of action he proposed to take toward a beast, so large, so terrifying, and unpredictable. He hesitated to answer, and then said judiciously, 'I think I shall praise it.'" I may not have been as judicious as that captain, but Swartz was a formidable player and good for the team. I cheered him from the bench, my heart healing a little each day.

But it was basketball with and without Richie Swartz that I had in mind when I began this, especially basketball's élan and its connection to writing poetry. As a former jump shooter with some ability, I remember what it was like to "get in a rhythm," to become "unstoppable," that feeling that the ball could not help but go in because you had entered the realm of magic, a place that was both yours and beyond you. I have a clear memory, even though the event took place over twenty-five years ago, of the evening I scored 45 points. I was a few years out of college, and I was playing in the *Long Island Press* League, which had teams composed of players like me, a combination of has-beens and almost-beens—a decent league, we used to think. I still see the box score as it appeared in the *Press* the next day. Dunn: 20 field goals, 5 foul shots, 45 points. I often had scored 20 points or so, but never 40. I missed very few shots that night and was aided by a childhood friend, a teammate, another Richie, who recognized early that some kind of magic was occurring. He passed the ball to me at exactly the right moments in exactly the right places (*my* places) on the court. Such an evening wouldn't have happened without him. I could liken him now to my perfect reader, historically equipped and presently attuned to understand my best stuff. His name was Richie Goldstein. Henceforth to be known as the good Richie.

I tell this story not to brag about my prowess, though I admit to a certain pride in the telling. I'm mostly interested in discussing what it means to be hot, those happy moments, to quote myself, when "practice and talent metamorphose / into a kind of ease." On that evening I was better than myself. Every previous hour on a basketball court, all my muscle memory, all my ability, converged that evening with dream. In fact I had dreamed, had visions, of such an evening. Every kid who's ever played has had such visions. "Unconscious," someone said afterward. "That guy was unconscious."

That I was. And long to be. Perhaps basketball and poetry have just a few things in common, but the most important is the possibility of transcendence. The opposite is labor. In writing, every writer knows when he or she is laboring to achieve an effect. You want to get from here to there, but find yourself willing it, forcing it. The equivalent in basketball is aiming your shot, a kind of strained and usually ineffective purposefulness. What you want to be is in some kind of flow, each next moment a discovery. Unconscious? Maybe, but more accurately a movement toward higher consciousness, of saying what you didn't know you could say, propelled by the mysteries of the process. The hot basketball player, however, has a distinct short-term advantage over the hot poet. He did it. Everybody knows he did it. The Nobel Committee need not meet to decide on it in private session. This is why scoring 45 points is more vivid in my memory than the writing and completion of any single poem. And why poets are often tormented. Yes, they might write successful, brilliant poems. But so few others agree or even care that they did. The fans don't stream into the studios and the garrets.

I think every poet needs two Richies—one to come up against, the other to act as a muse. The tradition in all its forbidding excellence is what the serious poet engages, consciously or unconsciously, every time he or she sits down to write. It can be as seminal as it is daunting. To have had a Richie Swartz in my basketball life may have prepared me to score 45 points some years later. Certainly to have had the good Richie on that magical night was to have had an inspiriting agent—I almost said angel. "I did it myself." That's the comment of the poet insufficiently respectful of mystery, not to mention his forebears.

I've always been pleased, though not surprised, that so many of the best basketball players are intelligent. They understand the demands of a given situation, they do with their abilities what is necessary for the team, much as a good poet learns not to dazzle unless it contributes to the entire poem. Lesser poets and lesser basketball players never seem to learn that lesson. Not to pass the ball to the open man, for example, has many corollaries in poetry writing, all of them equally self-indulgent. To love a line too much because you wrote it, even though it doesn't work in the poem. Or to put in a poem something that happened to you, whether you've made a place for it or not.

It's lovely to watch a team yield to the temporary brilliance of a particular player. A good team will always adjust to someone with a hot hand, will know that it's in their interest to get the ball to that person, as Richie Goldstein did in my case. Similarly, a poem might have to expand to accommodate an important discovery. The poet's job always is to find a livable home for what he's found himself saying or doing. If he can't, he needs to save the wonderful discovery for another occasion, or abandon it entirely. "Court sense," basketball pundits call it. I know some poets who don't have it.

Wallace Stevens in his poem "On Modern Poetry" talks about "sudden rightnesses, wholly / containing the mind, below which it cannot descend, / beyond which it has no will to rise." When the networks replay great moments such as Julius Erving's driving, swooping layup, or any of Michael Jordan's acrobatics, we have instances of sudden rightnesses, clearly recognizable. Announcers often loosely call these moments a kind of poetry, which may be accurate in the Stevens sense: utterly sufficient. But I worry about such locutions in our culture, which so often trivializes poetry. Too many poems are reduced by their readers to a single meaning, capsulized into catchphrases, distilled into information. Poetry's sudden rightnesses exist within larger contexts, and are right because of what precedes and follows them. They may be extractable, but at a cost. Here, basketball and its quick pleasures are part of a national problem: the short attention span, the quick, uncontemplative take. Poems are often demanding because they are trying to be equal to the complexities of the world and how it feels to be alive in it.

I've learned something about sudden rightnesses from basketball as well as from poetry. But poetry alone has slowed me down, taught me patience and the rewards of contemplation. There are reasons why people don't exchange high-fives in libraries. Poetry teaches you to say yes quietly—and at its best it doesn't let you escape from experience, from the hard business of living. To be a poetry fan you have to be prepared to wince, to have some of your shibboleths subverted. If you're a true fan, nothing again will ever be satisfactorily reduced to the thrill of victory, the agony of defeat. "Works of art," as Camus reminded us, "are not born in flashes of the imagination, but in daily fidelity."

Now I only play basketball when my brother comes to visit, two or three times a year. Out of old habit we get the ball, go to the schoolyard, and play one-on-one. He's forty-nine, three years younger than I, and he almost always wins. Our abilities are so comic that we hold and bump a lot, and there's not a move that either of us has that the other hasn't seen a thousand times. "What to make of a diminished thing," Frost says. Indeed.

I like to think of Richie Swartz this way, maybe with a bum leg, fat, out on some schoolyard, just trying to keep something that was good and felt good intact. Who knows, maybe he hasn't lost a step, as Odysseus never does in rereadings. After all, he's Richie Swartz. Whatever his condition, something of his transcendent past must come back to him. Sweet moves and the ball in the hole; nothing like it. Well, almost nothing. It's something you don't forget, and with luck by the time you're fifty you've replaced it with something else, or can settle for the vicarious. Without luck . . . God knows, those old battlefield stories are legendary.

My brother and I play until we're exhausted, a stage soon reached. Each of us has usually made at least one shot that brings back a semblance of the old powers. Two such shots can create delusions of a major order. At dinner, we're likely to replay those moments. Our wives exchange the glances of grown-ups bemused by their children. But neither of them ever corkscrewed into the paint, double-clutched, and kissed the ball just right off the backboard.

TWO THINGS YOU NEED

BALLS TO DO

A Miscellany from a Former Professional
Basketball Player Turned Poet

NATALIE DIAZ

THE BASKETBALL COURT = THE PAGE

Buzzer beaters and miracle shots are nonexistent in poetry—every poem I've heaved into the mail with more prayer than craft or confidence has been off the mark.

Worse than a poem full of hot air, an air ball.

UNIFORMS

You need one to play pro ball.

Vs.

You can write in only your undies, or in a coffee-stained Allman Brothers Concert T-shirt, or, better yet, in nothing more than a housecoat and dark socks, sans sports bra . . . no one cares.

Once you're issued a uniform on a professional basketball team, you're an official professional.

Vs.

Until you publish a book, you're in a developing league, i.e., playing for love of the game.

TRUTH

You can exaggerate, embellish, imagine or lie about what happens in a poem, and it is preferable.

Vs.

In basketball, a man or woman in black and white stripes blows a whistle that translates to, "Yeah, right. You know you slapped her arm. I saw you."

Some athletes in the NBA are known as "players" because of their philandering ways. Some poets are "players" also, especially at AWP.

Basketball, like poetry, is a universal language, but not yet like fiction or *fútbol*, but we're working on it.

The matter of traveling: (*a*) in poetry, it is encouraged, (*b*) in basketball, it will land you on the bench, which brings us to the matter of sitting: (*a*) again, highly encouraged in poetry, (*b*) not so great in basketball, regardless of whether it's on a bench or in a chair, sitting means you're not in the game—Pine Time is No Time.

Solitariness: (*a*) a must for writing poetry, (*b*) technically speaking, it's not possible to play basketball alone (however, some people are much better when they have no opponents).

Suicides: (*a*) not good for poets, ever (*b*) never good for basketball players, either.

FOULS = REJECTION LETTERS

BUT in poetry, you don't have to keep track of the # you accumulate, which is a good thing for some of us. (If there is a rejection letter limit, I'd rather not know.)

The matter of Rejection Letters: Sure they hurt. They bruise the ego a little. This is where basketball comes in handy—Remember the reservation pickup game mottos: "No Blood, No Foul," and, "You're either hurt, or you're injured." If your fingers aren't broken, if you're nose isn't bleeding, get back out there. Plus, getting your three-point shot blocked (aka rejected, stuffed, swatted, packed, sent packing, denied, shut-down, knocked-down-to-size, faced, etc.) into the third row by Chamique Holdsclaw in the NCAA Finals, in front of over 30,000 people, and on national TV, while the entire reservation back home is gathered in front of the casino big screens waiting for you to make them proud, is so-much-worse than having *The New Yorker* reject you quietly, politely, over the privacy of your e-mail (even though you were obviously shooting out of your range). Another thing: in basketball, no one will give you cryptic pointers about your shot, like "Memorable, but needs culling."

INJURIES

I have torn my ACL, MCL, and meniscus (the unhappy triad), fractured my leg and wrist (not at the same time), severed a blood vessel under my eye socket that gave me a black eye for an entire year, suffered a concussion or two, jammed my fingers several hundred times, a little plantar fasciitis, gritted my teeth through IT-Band Syndrome and cortisone shots in abundance, pulled muscles, sprained ankles that I still have nightmares about—all playing a game, basketball.

Vs.

Once, I was rushing to the post office to make a postmark deadline and I stubbed my toe on the curb out front.

SIMILARITIES

I sweat a lot when I play ball. I sweat a lot when I write poetry.

The cost of basketball shoes, which need to be replaced every few months (if you are playing the right way, the hard way), is equal to the amount you'll spend on contests.

WHICH BRINGS ME TO CONTESTS:

For those of us "retirees," the absence of the thrill of competition has left us hungry and desperate. I am, to my detriment, a contest junkie, often foregoing open submissions because I am determined to win something, ANYTHING, one last time. It's not the prize money I'm after, it's that glitzy little word: WINNER.

I've stooped so low as to only apply for fellowships at universities that my college basketball team beat during my playing days. This way, if I'm rejected, at least I have the satisfaction of knowing that one time, not long ago, I was the winner.

Another similarity: I used to be a champ at playing H-O-R-S-E, and I recently wrote a poem about a horse.

NOSTALGIA

I know I can't fill the void that basketball has left, but some days when I rise from my desk chair and feel shooting pain in my knees (which are not yet thirty in poetry-years, but in basketball-years are ancient) and creaking in other joints, I recognize these aches as close to what I once had. And every now and then, I let go of a line or an image and know instantly, as soon as it rolls from the curve of my mind or my gut, that it's going in, that it won't rattle around the rim, it won't brick-up and fall short or bounce too hard from the backboard, that it won't fall flat on the page . . . and it's smooth and sure and turns the net to flames, and as much as I want to stand and watch it, and pat myself on the ass for how beautiful it is, I know I have to keep moving on down the page.

THE SIMPLE RHYMES OF DEFENSE

GARY FINCKE

Lee Pierce looked like he knew his way around. When he stopped to speak to the guard at the initial Western Penitentiary checkpoint, Pierce told him who we were instead of requesting directions. "The Scared Straight basketball team," my office mate voice-overed, citing a show that had made a small stir a few years before. "I'm pretty sure we're all going to change our ways after this."

A couple of guys laughed, but I didn't. I was uneasy already, coming to play basketball at what I knew was a prison for men who'd committed more serious crimes than DUI and delinquent child support, what accounted for most of the population in the county lockup where we all lived thirty miles north. Pierce, who coached the team at our two-year campus, had thought it would be an interesting way to spend a Sunday afternoon in early February. "What else do you have to do now that the Super Bowl is over?" he'd said.

We crossed from one gate to another, cutting through a field of dirt packed so hard it wasn't even muddy at a time of year when my yard was sopping wet from melting snow. It could have been mistaken for a parking lot if there weren't goalposts. "No pads allowed," my office mate said, keeping up his patter. He had a PhD in geology but mostly taught geography at our two-year campus, a course designed for would-be teachers that included a test that asked them to fill in the names of all the states on an otherwise blank map. "No helmets," he kept on. "The Gerald Ford bulldogs." I was hoping he'd shut up before we encountered our first prisoner.

By the time we reached the prison locker room, I had shown my comb and keys to four men and had heard three gates slam exactly as if the guards believed we were a team hired by mobsters to initiate an escape. Because my contact lens case had only been opened twice, I estimated it was half as difficult to smuggle dope as it was to transport weapons, but I kept that observation to myself.

The locker room had a bus-station men's room aura that hurried all of us into our gear. "How many diseases can you catch from a toilet seat?" my office mate asked, but this time nobody laughed or even offered a guess, and I was pleased.

Pierce had brought along one nonfaculty player, an associate degree student who looked to be in his midtwenties and in shape. I didn't mind having somebody who would hustle back on defense once my legs were gone. And I especially was glad the other phys ed professor besides Pierce was a former lineman at West Virginia, somebody with the bulk and the instincts to clear out the lane and rebound no matter what sort of men were on the other team.

Not a bad pickup team for a bunch of professors. I'd once been a second-string college player, and Pierce had played college games when the score was close enough to make his contributions matter. Even the first guy off the bench, a math professor, had played small-college ball, and he was all about hustle, slapping wrists and tugging jerseys and diving to the floor for loose balls. But that was it. The other three guys who'd made the trip were standard-order college faculty talent, guys who picked up their dribble as soon as the defense showed up, who led with their eyes when they passed, who shot and watched the result while their men released and cherry-picked for layups. Worse, none of them could run half as long as I could.

As soon as we entered the gym, I fixed on the fan-shaped iron backboards. I hadn't played at baskets like these since I'd been too small to shoot anything from outside the foul line and was at home on the grade-school playground. It looked to me as if a short jump shot meant to kiss high off glass would miss this armor and land on the support. I lofted a twelve-footer and sure enough, I hit the edge. I shot from fifteen feet along the baseline and produced an air ball in front of the rim. Pierce didn't seem to notice my anxiety or that of anyone else. He was excited, slapping our backs and chasing loose balls. I thought he might be using this afternoon game as a way of putting aside the nine-game losing streak his team was in the midst of.

I was glad the gym was empty except for two guards. I had time, maybe, to get acclimated. One thing I didn't have to worry about was the thinly padded wall behind the basket. I wasn't about to drive the lane through traffic inside a prison. Let the math teacher break his neck. I moved in to ten feet and tried different angles. The court was so narrow I didn't think I'd get much off from the corners anyway.

The prisoner team jogged in through a door opposite us, escaping a locker room I didn't even want to imagine. I was sure each one of my teammates was absorbing two things: all of the prisoners were black; one of them was a life-size replica of the NBA's man-child, Darryl Dawkins.

What else I noticed? After giving us the once-over in return, none of the convicts acted as if they expected us to make this game interesting.

I felt the same way. Players no taller than my six feet two loped to the basket and jammed the ball through with ease. The big guy, despite his bulk, casually crushed a slam back over his head. "You'll get a poem out of this," Pierce said. "Won't you?" He'd asked me once why what I wrote were called poems if none of them rhymed. Standing near the foul line with a ball cradled absently against my chest, it was all I could do to grunt "maybe" so he wouldn't ask again.

Two side doors opened, and the crowd filed in, every one of them black as well. It was a sociology lesson. Every guard that accompanied them was as white as we were. My Jim Crow legs felt heavy and soggy, but Pierce, apparently, was blind. He wound right into his pregame speech as if the other end of the court was dotted with clean-shaven, cowlicked farm boys. "We managed to get a game with their A team," Pierce said. "I talked you guys up enough to get a real challenge."

Right about then I didn't want a challenge. I wanted the B or even the C team out there for the jump ball—five white guys with bad hands and no wind, the kind of team that would drop back into a sagging zone and concede my eighteen-foot jump shot with only a few waves of its tattooed arms. Pierce was an idiot to have claimed we were anything but overeducated. Certainly, I could see clearly that all of my swearing and beer-swilling in college had done nothing but camouflage my innate gutlessness.

For the opening tip, the convicts sent out a thin, twitchy guy who looked to be about five foot nine. Our West Virginia football alum was about six foot five, but he didn't get much air under his sneakers. The stands buzzed approval for what looked to be the first of many humiliations, and they got their wish when the little guy cleanly tapped the ball to the Darryl Dawkins look-alike. He whirled and found a teammate who drove uncontested to the basket, but because that guy, who looked to be my size, turned a 180 and tried to jam behind his head, the ball banged off the back rim and carried directly to my office mate. From where I stood, not having moved since the ball had left the referee's hands, I trotted down court as if all of this had been choreographed.

For six minutes, incredibly, we built a lead: 14–6, the scoreboard read, and the convicts took a timeout. They were leading in righteous moves and attempted dunks, but no one had taken a routine shot. Worse, they were going for every head fake as if they were chemistry professors anticipating the first clean block of their lives during a lunchtime scrimmage. And somehow I'd hit three out of four from medium range, rising to shoot while the guy guarding me was falling back to earth.

"Anybody winded?" Pierce said in the huddle. The math guy was bouncing. Somebody along the bench said, "We're kicking their asses" so loudly I worried the A team might have heard.

As it turned out, the team that returned for the convicts had enlarged itself. Now they had three enforcers inside and two serious-looking guys outside, one of which, when I made my one move—fake left, go right, and pull up—never flinched. He slapped at the ball, catching my wrist, but there was no call. I had to let my shot go without getting my feet squared, and barely caught iron. "Shit, white bread," the guy said, following me down court like a shadow, "you been read."

The prisoners set up a series of picks, delivering forearms, throwing hips: everything away from the ball. There was only one referee, and they freed cutters for layups until it was 16–16 and Pierce made an emphatic T with his hands. "You drowning now, white bread," my shadow said as we turned toward our benches. "You in over your head."

The math guy was up and ready. "Okay," Pierce declared, "you're in. We need somebody to fight through screens. We need some hustle. We need some get-up-and-go."

Two minutes later we were down by seven, and I had the ball stripped and slam-dunked through what was, by now, the far distant basket. "You dead, white bread," my shadow said so softly I thought for a moment he was being kind. Only the math guy chased after, so he tried a long baseball pass that was intercepted, and he found himself facing a two-on-one, the second slam in eight seconds bouncing off his shoulder as the gym rocked with high-fives. "Yo, bread," I heard to my left a few seconds later, so I turned right and fed the math guy, who went on a kamikaze run at the hoop, getting the ball tipped from the side so it bounced against a knee and caromed loose in the lane.

The convicts' big guy surged out of the crowd with it—no surprise—but he was holding his eye as if he could feel pain. "Motherfucker!" he yelled, and swung an elbow that caught the jump-ball artist flush, snapping his head back and laying him out on the floor. "Motherfucker!" the big guy roared again, and everybody backed off, opening a circle around what looked to be a dead man.

Pierce managed to keep his coach's reflexes. He motioned us to the bench. I sat down first and said, "I'm beat" at once. "Put somebody in."

"Somebody go in for me," Pierce said. "I'm the one poked the big fella in the eye."

"They have one cold-cocked guy out there," my office mate offered. "They have themselves an incident."

The downtime stretched. The Darryl Dawkins guy walked to the bench, covering one eye like a man taking a vision test on the move. Soon only the unconscious player was left on the court. When I picked up some movement in the bleachers behind me, I stood up like I'd found my second wind, but it was only two prison guards stationing themselves in the open row between us and the crowd that looked, suddenly, like a comically ineffective moat.

The downed player began to make pedaling motions with his legs as the referee approached Pierce. "You want to call it a day?" he said.

Instead of taking a vote, Pierce said, "No way."

"I can't protect you out there," the referee confessed. "I can't guarantee anything."

Pierce nodded. "We understand," he said, freely using the collective pronoun.

The recovering player was sitting up by now, shaking out the cobwebs. I imagined him listening to the buzz of a million trapped flies just before he stood and shuffled to the bench. "You be whooped now, white bread," I heard the first time I touched the ball. "Your woman good in bed?"

I wondered if Pierce, dribbling a few feet away, had heard. There was poetry he recognized here all right, but for me, by then, it was a narrative of difference, the metaphors of boundaries, including the one created by a phalanx of white prison guards. For the rest of the half I shot nothing but NBA-style three-pointers before I could get stripped again. We were down thirteen at the half, a testament to the convicts' inability to convert offensive rebounds.

Back in the locker room I watched a centipede as long as my thumb emerge from under a locker. There had to be more, I thought, though it was wise enough to retreat so only its head was visible. "We're in this thing," Pierce was ranting like Custer, but by now, except for the math instructor, there weren't any soldiers or schoolboys in the room with him.

"One of the guards protecting our backs said the big guy caved in somebody's head with a cue stick," my office mate said. "Manslaughter is what he's serving time for. He's up for parole in less than a year."

"Let's stall," I said. "Let's hold the ball until he's back in the world." In the silence that followed I noticed the centipede was gone.

"Let's listen to coach," the math professor said, and I stared at him, remembering that Pierce had once told me that he worked out every day, that he'd told Pierce his biggest fear, at thirty-two, was getting out of shape.

"Come on," he said again, "let's do it for coach," and Pierce slapped him on the back.

"Corn bread," I thought, but the rhyme didn't come to me.

With five minutes left we were down by twenty-three, and Pierce emptied the bench. I sat down with fifteen points and one accidental rebound. We lost by thirty-four. The guards opened the doors for the crowd, and they filed out in a way that surprised me with its deference. I shook hands with three of the other players, missing the guy who'd called me out with simple rhymes. He'd disappeared before I'd dragged myself off the bench where I'd listened to Pierce shout encouragement to the makeshift team he'd put on the floor.

I didn't chance my bare feet on the floor of the gang shower. I toweled off as best I could and turned everything in my locker inside out and shook it before I put it back on.

Outside it was snowing. Just flurries, but threatening worse, Sunday afternoon turned dismal, dark clouds amplifying the twilight of February's early sunset. I waited until my office mate slid into the car Pierce was driving, then opened the door of the other. I'd heard enough chatter for one day.

When my next thought was that I felt released, I was embarrassed for myself. The driver, a computer science instructor, worried aloud about whether the road might turn slick. As soon as he turned on the radio to search for a forecast, the trivial words of a set of sponsors welcomed me back into the world.

BASKETBALL AND POETRY

Strange Bedfellows

MARGARET GIBSON AND DAVID MCKAIN

MARGARET: DAVID MCKAIN AND I MET AT YADDO IN THE SUMMER OF 1975. I lived in Washington, D.C., and taught at George Mason University, where I had come up for tenure a year early but hadn't received it. In fact, I didn't really feel I had tenure anywhere. My first marriage had ended two years earlier, my housemate had recently married, and I was moving out of the house we'd shared for a year or more, and her husband was moving in. I was making new friends, and I had a first book in the making, but I was also settling into being someone who spent a lot of time riding around the beltway of D.C., commuting from the city where I lived to the suburb where I worked. Does anyone feel at home on the beltway? I'd arrived gratefully at Yaddo, eager for time alone, time to write. I was ready, I told myself, to begin life truly on my own. My new poems were telling me that.

So why was I, the third morning there, pausing at the mail table to study the list of guests, trying to figure out which of the three *Davids* listed was the one I'd met, whose last name I now wanted to know? "You must be interested in him," I observed to myself.

That night David McKain and I went dancing with a group of others. Perhaps because we knew our time together at Yaddo was brief—we overlapped by only a week, and then he would return to Connecticut, to his two children, to the house in the woods he'd built himself once his marriage had ended, to his tenured job at the University of Connecticut—we made the most of the dancing. We danced until they closed the place down, and we talked the rest of the night. Intimacy and candor came easily. The rest of the week, we worked on our poems in our separate quarters. But during the hours after 4:00 P.M. we were constantly together, and we knew we would be together for the rest of our lives. "Just don't get married in the Rose Garden here at Yaddo," Polly Hanson advised. "None of those marriages lasted."

I shocked my department chair at George Mason when I called to resign. "You've known him *how long?*" he asked. "Don't resign. Take a year's leave without pay. You can always come back. Give yourself a safety net." I couldn't really explain why I was making this move; it certainly wasn't anything I'd planned. It just felt right. Even so, I was a little embarrassed to leave my job so abruptly, saying . . . *I met a man.* Wasn't I betraying the feminist in me? "You are; I am," I told myself. But it *felt right,* much as the new poems that were coming at Yaddo *felt right.* I was finally, I told myself, speaking my own voice, living my own life. And the Richmond rule book I'd been given for life? I'd tossed it over my shoulder along with the feminist one.

Poetry brought us together—the muse our guardian angel? Perhaps. But from the first evening together at Yaddo we already knew that there were other deep ties, in our family backgrounds and in our early religious training—and in our departures from that training—in our interest in meditative practice, and in our politics. David was, far more than I, adventurous. Sometimes, I thought, I just don't know what he's going to do next—and that excited me.

Perhaps couples focus at first on what draws them together, what they have in common. We spent hours reading each other's poems, making suggestions, beginning the difficult work of honesty and tact and commitment. We talked of writing a book together. We bought a house; I began to know and love his children; we got married.

We got married, and, then, I discovered to my surprise in January of that first season together, we watched basketball. "*Basketball?*" my D.C. friend Kay echoed with a strong interrogative. "Well, you're tall," she laughed. We both laughed. But basketball was one of the passions of David's life—the UConn Huskies in particular. I had married, I came to understand, a former basketball scholarship recipient, a member of the freshman team at the University of Connecticut.

To save heating costs, we watched the UConn games from our bed, under the covers, snuggling in a cold room. What I remember from watching basketball under the covers is, well, what you remember from under the covers. But I also remember a single visual image: little Joey Welton, the point guard, coming down the court, dribbling for all he was worth, his pageboy bob bobbing, the ball bouncing in surprising ways before he looked right and passed left. Mesmerized, I watched the hair bob, the ball bounce. It reminded me of watching the movie screen during intermission at the Byrd theater in Richmond, during Eddie Weaver's organ recitals, when the words to popular songs would flash up on the screen for the audience to sing, and a little ball bounced from syllable to syllable to guide the audience in the sing-along. Without knowing it, already I was linking basketball and poetry, transforming the basketball hitting the floor into the white ball that stressed syllables. I was learning to sing along.

Whatever I knew of basketball as a game lay in the recesses of gym period at St. Catherine's School in Richmond, Virginia. We played a half-court game then, because "girls weren't as strong as boys," and we shouldn't get winded. The rules were different. I never "saw" the court. I never developed "a sense of where you are." I rarely scored. We wore little yellow-skirted uniforms with bloomers underneath. I remember the bloomers. I was tall, but I never made the varsity team, nor did I want to—I'd rather be home, reading.

Married to David, I worked on poems in the morning; winter evenings, I watched UConn basketball with one eye open.

David: Basketball and poetry are connected in my life. I didn't realize that until I left the Allegheny Mountains in Bradford, Pennsylvania, and in the fall of 1955 entered college at the University of Connecticut where, fortunately, I had been awarded a basketball scholarship. I wasn't as surprised to have a scholarship as I should have been, even though my earliest success had occurred on the basketball court, when at the age of fourteen, I scored 37 points, playing in a game for the Class-A Town League with a cast on my right foot. I wouldn't know then that I was playing basketball with a passion and enthusiasm that welled up from a place deep inside me, as similarly I would teach poetry many years later when I had college students to teach. I never thought I'd be a teacher. I never thought I'd go to college, much less read poetry. The rhythm that dominated my early life was the rhythm I lived on the basketball court in Bradford—and also in Harlem.

I had spent two summers in Harlem playing basketball in the parks and on the streets of Morningside Heights in the shadow of the Church of the Master, where my mother played the organ during the summer, and I was left to fend for myself, the only white kid in the neighborhood. Being white in Harlem made me an outsider; so did my small-town roots. I was getting used to changes in those summers, and playing basketball was the one stable part of my life.

In Bradford, expelled from several academic classes and sent to the library, then kicked out of the library, I'd had time on my hands during school hours, and I'd spent much of my time in the Bradford High School gym, shooting hoops with one other outsider and troublemaker, a kid who said, "It ain't so bad, Dave." Perhaps because of those hours of nearly solitary practice, I learned to shoot foul shots in a manner that was, if accurate, unconventional. Coach Wilcox wasn't impressed with my style or with the results. He wanted me to shoot the basketball in the way he advised. But I couldn't make hoops when I shot the ball his way. Challenged by him, I went to the line, and, insisting on shooting the ball my way, I made fifty foul shots in a row. After that, to his credit, Coach never interfered with me. He even praised me.

But I graduated number 285 in a class of 300, and I had no plans or prospects other than working in an ice cream factory in Bradford. I would not remember—and it's possible I didn't even know until years later—that I'd been awarded a poetry prize my senior year. I was an outsider; one didn't expect recognition for poetry. Poems were written *in, of,* and *for* the moment. They moved, as life did, in surprising shifts of direction.

That summer my life changed its direction. My mother fed me the ball, so to speak. She was returning to Harlem; instead of traveling with her, I was to spend the summer in Storrs, Connecticut, with my uncle Walter McKain, a sociology professor, and with his large family. I have written of that transition in my memoir, *Spellbound: Growing up in God's Country,* and I cull from those passages here:

I had been talking with my uncle Walter, who, after some tales of my troubled father as a boy, turned and asked me seriously, "What are you going to do this fall?"

"I don't know," I answered warily. I suspected that he had been talking with my mother.

He laughed good-naturedly as though I had made a joke. I did not know why he laughed, but his laughter was infectious. "I spoke to Mr. Richards about you today," he said. "The dean of admissions. He said you could go over and take an exam. Mr. Greer said something, too. I don't know. Some exam to see if you can get in."

Mr. Greer was the head basketball coach, a white-haired gentleman who looked like a senator. Uncle Walter said he never raised his voice during a game and that was why people called him a gentleman. Coach Greer had asked me over to scrimmage one Saturday on the court outside his house. We had played three-on-three, and I guarded Richie Kiernon, last year's starting varsity guard. Richie had hair in the hollow of his neck below his Adam's apple and he wore a St. Christopher's medal. The other five players were on the varsity, too, a team that had finished the previous season among the top twenty in the country. Each of the players wore a ring with NIT in gold letters across a ruby. After we scrimmaged, Coach Greer shook my hand and said I had played well. He said he would be in touch.

"What kind of exam?" I asked my uncle.

"A special exam to see if you can do college-level work. It's tomorrow at one o'clock if you want to take it. You can take the car." He turned the book over on his lap, took off his glasses, and looked at me. "This is sort of a second chance, you know. You want it, don't you?"

"Yes," I said cheerfully, not wanting to appear ungrateful, but I was not sure what I wanted.

The car he let me drive was a 1928 Ford, a jalopy everyone in the family called the "Putt-Bang." Since the car had no top, chickens hopped in at night and roosted under the dashboard, and if no one had used the car earlier, the chickens were still there after lunch. They squawked and flapped their wings when I opened the door, lifting themselves just high enough to clear the rumble seat, then thudding back to earth, bouncing like huge winged cabbages in the dirt.

Dean Richards sat behind a stack of neat papers and smiled through the heat wave, in control. His fingernails were manicured, and he wore a freshly ironed shirt, a narrow bow tie, and a light gray suit. Short and trim, he made me nervous.

"How is the basketball team going to fare next year?" he asked dutifully.

"I don't know," I said with an embarrassed smile.

"I've heard good things about your game, David," he said, but it was obvious he did not care much about basketball.

He glanced at his pocket watch. "Well, I have ten after. Let's find an empty room."

We walked up three flights of stairs to a cubbyhole just wide enough for a desk and a chair: Mr. Richards handed me a packet of papers wrapped in plastic. He looked at his watch again, handed me two freshly sharpened pencils, and said he would be back at 3:15.

Without air-conditioning and on the top floor, the small room was stifling. As soon as he was gone, I opened the window and leaned out over a parking lot. The sun clanged off the chrome bumpers and the windshields: the heat and glare made me dizzy. A man stood in front of his car with his hands on his hips and kicked gravel. His hood was up, his engine steaming. Beyond were cornfields, a meadow, and a long slope called Horse Barn

Hill. A mustard haze hung over everything, and, to my surprise, I began to cry.

For the first time I realized how much I did not want to pour cement and get married right away, whether I passed the exam or not—and I did not want to play basketball in the City League either, not even for Fishkin Clothiers, the city champs. I blew my nose, broke open the seal of the exam, straightened my chair, and did not look up until the dean rapped at the door two hours later.

I had been lucky. The next day I learned I had scored in the top 5 percent of those in the nation who had taken the exam, an exam that measured potential rather than performance. The score meant a great deal to me. I was not a "dummy." Dean Richards called it "a calculated risk for all concerned," but I would be attending the University of Connecticut on a basketball scholarship.

A week before school opened Coach Greer introduced me to other members of the team. The varsity was made up of older guys who had been in the Korean War. At twenty-six Gordon Ruddy was nine years older than I. The other members of the team were all in their twenties. Gordon said that, according to *The New York Times,* we had the best freshman basketball team in the country.

"In the country?" I asked in disbelief.

"Sure, that's what it said. But don't forget, that's only freshman. When you play us, it's all over." Gordon smiled menacingly then became quite friendly again, gentle. "I was only kiddin'," he said.

We were all standing around joking, but I could not get rid of the nagging thought that I did not belong on the best freshman basketball team in the country. Other guys from Bradford played better ball than I did, and yet there I was living next to Marco Malone, one of the stars on the varsity. With his soft, deft hands, Marco could make shots from all over the court.

Basketball at Connecticut was really like a full-time job. Practice lasted most of the afternoon, from three o'clock right on through supper. Only the most disciplined students were able to stay in school and play basketball at the same time. I was at a disadvantage. I did not know where to begin. I was trying to learn how to study while everyone else was studying. (End of excerpt from *Spellbound*.)

Again, I was on the outside. I was on the outside as much as the African American kids on the freshman team who came up to me in practice and said, "You said you were in Harlem some summers. You know a kid named Turner?" I did know Turner. Not from the block where I lived in Harlem. I'd met him on his turf, and he'd taken me under his wing, showing me the ropes. He was an angry, sweet guy, and I'd been grateful for his help, much as I'd been for the help of another friend who'd walk the streets with me, saying, "Let's cross here," when he spotted kids ahead he knew would pick fights with me because I didn't belong. Now here I was at UConn, an outsider making friends with other outsiders who knew Turner.

I'd signed up to be a business major because I didn't know what else to do—and perhaps because business in the midfifties seemed to be at the center of things. But during the second semester of my freshman year, I developed mono and was again spending time outside of classes—spending time alone. But now I had books to read, *Sons and Lovers* for one. I read books of poems, too. When I returned to campus the following year, I'd made two decisions. I left basketball; I quit business. I signed up as an English major, a reader of books, a reader of Eliot and Pound, Ginsberg, Lowell, and that elegant outsider, Cavafy.

Basketball brought me to college; college brought me to poetry.

Margaret: And poetry, after Yaddo, brought me to live in a house in the woods. The natural, or the living, world came rushing into my poems. I gardened, I roamed the ridges of the woodlands and wetlands, I took long walks in the afternoon.

The physical activity that precedes, or underlies, my poems certainly isn't playing basketball—it's walking, mostly solitary walking. I walk and walk until breath fills my head, thoughts empty out, and I come to rest—now and again—in a clearing. Out in the open, my looking and observing turns to *seeing*. Then I may feel the pulse of an inner rhythm, see or sense an image, think in metaphor, find a word or phrase (or it finds me), and I begin to move with it. The natural rhythm of the English language, as Wordsworth knew, is iambic; walking is iambic, until the terrain forces the foot into spondee or trochee, or until one lopes along in anapests trying to keep up (I do try) with my husband's longer stride or with our dog's dodge and weave through the understory.

Watching basketball, not having ever truly played the game, I'm a spectator of movement, much of it surprising: look left, pass right. For years, unsure of the rules, I'd follow a mass of bodies, picking one player to follow, then two at a time, then perhaps I'd "see" a play unfold, a strategy foiled or embodied. I'd watch a player like UConn's Ray Allen move constantly, staying or getting open.

A sucker for the spectacular, I'd be amazed at Larry Bird or Magic Johnson, I'd thrill to the airborne leaps of Michael Jordan, I'd "study" the choreography of the fast break. Watching the spectacular leap to stuff the ball or the ingenious surprise of a backhanded pass, I was awed—amazed at the skill of a well-taught instrument, the human body itself, magnified and transfigured, transformed from the awkward amble into a powerful mastery of movement.

> And isn't that what we want, to be taken
> out of a sentence into the air, where conversation
> blossoms into speechlessness . . .

asks poet Phyllis Levin.

Watching basketball, sometimes I'd remember snatches of poems:

> My heart in hiding
> Stirred for a bird,—the achieve of, the mastery of the thing!

> Brute beauty and valor and act, oh, air, pride, plume here
> Buckle! AND the fire that breaks from thee then, a billion
> Times told lovelier, more dangerous. . . .

I began to see each player as a person AND as a kind of movement or rhythm—or as Hopkins again puts it:

> Each mortal thing does one thing and the same:
> Deals out that being indoors each one dwells;
> Selves—goes itself; myself it speaks and spells,
> crying, *What I do is me: for that I came.*

Surely anyone watching a greatly skilled and inspired basketball player, or reading a poem by a greatly skilled and inspired poet, has felt the truth of those lines. For each player, body and mind, "What I do is me: for that I came." And the sheer wonder of it: how can he (Bird, Johnson, Jordan) or she (Sue Bird, Diana Taurasi) DO *that?* It's the rapt question of anyone who would be a maker or master craftsperson, who has worked at any craft, learning the rules in order to be released from their hold. Learning the craft in order to *be*, without self-consciousness, freed into a new rhythm, a heart-leaping, line-breaking fluidity I find only in poetry when I consider language and only in basketball when I consider sport.

Perhaps I love watching basketball because of the pure envy of seeing a player, now and again, fully at home in his or her own skin—living at the center of himself or herself—no longer an outsider. And I love poetry—writing it—for that occasional moment when the lines fall rapidly, purely: when it feels "as if" I'm out of my own way, *I am* the way the words sing as they sing themselves. I call it "liftoff." A basketball player might say that he or she is "in a zone." One is doing and being simultaneously, fully "not-knowing" in the sense of not scheming or thinking about it: the move just *feels right.*

David Waggoner writes of poetry that what "begins as a kind of game turns out to be the most complex and rewarding of all game-like activities, something more nearly religious, as demanding and baffling and compelling as ethics, metaphysics, the search for a god or even love." The game of basketball remains for me, by comparison, secular.

But then, I watch it; I don't play it.

I do let poetry play me; I do participate in that special way of "not-knowing" that may or may not lead to making a poem. Can a poet say how a poem—part craft, part inspiration—becomes a nod toward what we know of unitary being in the moment, fully alive in one's own skin? What feels right only comes after years of apprenticeship and practice. And even then there are errors, falterings, one misses the point—or the shot goes awry. But on occasion there is a way of moving and being that flowers from focus, attention, and readiness.

David and I have been teachers, writers, and walkers of the woods together for many years. We've watched basketball together, made love, baffled and respected and trusted each other, and now we're writing this essay together. Not all of our moves take us into a poem. Here, however, is a poem I wrote for David, about David. It says nothing about basketball directly. But it weaves about, trying to stay open; it looks right and passes left. It follows its own rhythm.

Notes in the Margin

When I pull down an old volume from the poetry shelves
and read, I find in the margin
your hasty scrawl—gists that might have become a poem

but remained hidden in the leaves of the book—like the
female tanager's muted green
sequestered among these tall summer oaks.

Canto XIII, Kung says: "And even I can remember a day
when historians left blanks
in their writing, I mean for things they didn't know . . ."

Then, off on a riff, you scrawled, *the honesty of hard
hands and oak trees
that split and buck back to take a man's arm . . .*

And I can see you back then on the old sofa, reading
in the evening, weary from clearing
trees for the house you were building in the woods.

*The power of a real tree allows a man to say, "I don't
know,"* you continued.
I think you must have frowned then, as you often do

when a thought matters, when it underscores the way
a body moves from
moment to moment, *not-knowing.* Over in the margin

your honesty deepens. *And I still don't know the boy
who lived back when mules
dragged logs and barges west, up the Canal.* And then

a leap—*I don't know the space within the dark basement
of a house built without a bulkhead cellar door.*
Beside the remaining cantos you must have also read,

you made no comment. Did you finish the poem you began
in the margins? What happened to
that boy? to the wide river? to the house whose cellar

kept its secrets hidden? And why do I want to know?
"Pull down thy vanity," Pound
chides. "Learn of the green world what can be thy place."

How lucky you are, my love, to have built a house,
cut wood, carried water.
You wanted a full life, a true heritage, built quietly

within. And it's not empty, your silence—it's ready.
When you walk out for the mail,
you forget yourself, and everything you know

disappears with you, as down the green lane, moving
in leafshade and sunspace,
the birds sing out their call notes, and you whistle back.

David: Agreed, a poem is a testament to solitude and reflection—but it's also a social document. Sometimes the game of basketball seems to me an apt metaphor for the ideal society, one with a common goal, with rules and bounds that guide the competition, and one which, within competition, fosters an opportunity for cooperation and creativity. The individual player can stand out, or he or she can perform in concert with others, doing the small, often unnoticed acts that benefit the whole team. Respect is earned by one's skill, one's steadiness, one's creativity. For me the glitz and the big salaries are distractions; the game's the thing.

Fully inside the game, no one's an outsider. Ironically the game of basketball—from pickup games on the street to Madison Square Garden—is one way those truly on the outs in our society can find a way "in." Perhaps playing basketball in Bradford and then again in Harlem gave me an inner template for *community,* for doing things with others, blending the competitive, the cooperative, and the creative. Certainly I've spent much of my adult life as a teacher, as a poet, as a citizen, looking for *community.*

As a team sport, at its best basketball cultivates values that poetry also cultivates: generosity, selflessness, and a self-confidence that *can* transcend egotism. Both basketball and poetry require us to play by the rules while creating new situations, new moves. Both are pursuits (of the word, of the ball) that expose our strengths and weaknesses; both challenge whatever you *thought* you knew, and insure that, in the flow, one is not an outsider. Poets look for metaphor and practice rhythmic speech; basketball, seen or played by a poet, can be a metaphor for living in the fully engaged momentum of life, "moment by moment, breath by breath"—as Margaret likes to say.

And, by the way, speaking of cooperation, let's write the last sentence of the essay together.

Margaret: Okay. Let's try.

David: In basketball, it's not the question of hitting the rhyme, but hitting the rim . . .

Margaret: and it's all about heading for that empty center:

Margaret and David: *Swish!*

BASKETBALL AND THE IMMIGRANT FAITH

PATRICK ROSAL

In 1986, when our bodies could do such things, four of us would contort into a Pontiac Fiero, a matchbox two-seater loaned to us by one of the gambling regulars. Our parents could play mah-jongg all night, the plastic tiles like the feet of a small flock of birds clacking on a roof. While our folks rotated seats at seven different tables in a three-day, all-day, all-night marathon of five- and twenty-dollar games (cursing each other and themselves in at least three languages), we'd head out, more often than not, to play basketball in the middle of the night.

Me and Jojo, the shorter pair of our quartet, had to straddle the gearshift together. Phil and Junji, a couple of six-footers, would pivot their shoulders a little toward the windows to make room for the full car ride. We could make the courts in under a half hour.

We were headed to The Ledge, a basketball court on campus at Rutgers that hung over Route 18 and peeked over the muddy Raritan River. Like no other courts in the area, there were lights there meant just for security, not for all-night games. The chain-link gates were sometimes locked, so one of us had to climb the twelve-foot fence and drop himself onto the other side, then let the rest of us in. In midwinter, we packed a couple shovels in the trunk to clear the slush. There were always slippery patches, small puddles of icy water, but we got it clean enough to run two-on-two.

I wasn't a particularly athletic kid to begin with, but my parents lobbied the principal to have me enter the first grade a year early, a kind of wish for precociousness that I never fully realized. I was smaller, slower, and more awkward than most of the kids throughout grade school. My parents came from a culture where one's physical work, farming and husbandry, kept one fit. In short, they were not athletes either. My dad claimed to have played basketball as a young man, so I was excited when one summer day he brought my older brother and me to the county college to shoot some hoops.

Having been shamed during gym by my lack of athleticism, this was my chance to maybe learn something from my dad. His thing was books, shelves and shelves of them. He had several advanced degrees in the humanities as well as a late-night local radio show for a short stint. I shouldn't have been surprised, then, when my dad, pushing fifty at the time, turned out to be a bigger version of my clumsy self with a basketball. Air balls and bricks lofted into the air, the trajectory of his shot launched from down between his bent knees. I remember feeling betrayed, resentful even, that my dad, who swore he knew the game, had no clue.

It was partially that indignation that drove me to learn the standards of the game. It was the feeling that a father—my father—had an obligation to teach me how to be among men. My friends were patient enough to let me run with them to learn some skills, but more than skills, I caught the fever, a chronic condition that heats you in the chest whenever you hear the round spank of a ball against the pavement. I was hooked.

Truth is, for me, there was almost nothing fun about basketball. Though I was eager for a run any time, anywhere, I was always the most serious dude on the court. I played hard. I ran hard, jumped, dribbled, and shot bricks hard. Of course, I fouled hard too, which meant I got fouled hard in return—big old hacks, body checks, elbows and bridges. In short, I didn't give a fuck. And if a play came to blows, well that was just another part of the game.

I was both reckless and sincere, each pickup game one more battle. That is to say, I knew intuitively that basketball meant something beyond itself. America's magnificence, more than mythically, resides in its abundance of utterly average people, and my parents, immigrants from the Philippines, wanted me to be American and therefore, I believed, average.

I did want to be American, but only if I could be extraordinary too. I was so utterly committed to basketball as a crucible not just of manhood, but an American manhood. Toward that goal, I was happy to spark your average pickup game into a neighborhood brawl. I didn't care if Phil, Junji, and Jo were my best friends in the world, which they were. If I couldn't win the game, then I'd make the game a fight and I'd win the fight instead.

To have grown up in that era, not just as an American of Asian descent, but particularly as a Filipino-American, meant growing up between worlds. English was one of the national languages of our parents. So in addition to speaking their provincial language in their hometowns, my parents were schooled not in the colonial language of England, but in the colonial language of America. You can see then how the expression *native tongue* confounds a Filipino's sense of home, or at least the ways in which a Filipino speaks about home and where we do or do not belong.

Academically, I was a gifted kid, though somewhat an underachiever. I just made it to a B average by the end of my senior year, flunking my Shakespeare final, just making the top third of the class at the all-boy Catholic high school I went to. That's the thing: I felt like I was constantly being measured up with standardized exams, rankings, GPAs, prodded with numbers and quotients, and like a real American teen, I called all of it bullshit.

Basketball, then, wasn't just a game; it was a way to have some agency, a way to be the one who tests—with one's own body—the likelihood and/or fictions of an American myth. And such tests happened in a *court,* from the Latin root meaning *an enclosed garden or yard,* a venue where sovereigns of the thirteenth century probably settled disputes.

The basketball court, unlike almost any other place I'd encounter in my adolescence, was the site where the complications of language didn't seem to burden the experience. This was Jersey, after all, and I'd grown up among working-class white folks, but also hopped the fence in the backyard to visit my friends on Manning Street, where most of the black families of the neighborhood lived. And just up the road was the Section 8 housing project where lived another group of friends who were one generation removed from the Bronx, two from Puerto Rico.

The New Jersey I came to love was a place where people didn't give a damn if you could diagram the modifier to a predicate, only how good you could D your man and pull up to nail an open ten-footer. Of course, on the court, speech was important as far as talking shit was important, and talking shit is the game, we all know, to which basketball is merely an adjunct.

So what, in god's name, was I scuffling for? The very English that I'd become proficient at in school, in and out of class, from the spelling bee whiz to the tattletale, was useless on the basketball court. I was no shit-talker, so with all those inside elbows late at night at The Ledge with my best friends, I was substituting something for speech.

I wasn't just practicing basketball; I was living a kind of life I couldn't the next morning, in the daylight, when I had to confront other young men, the ones who looked more like the America everyone seemed to believe in, the America that lettered in three sports and kissed his mother good-bye on the way to the bus and had a casserole waiting for him when he got home. So there I was, under the cover of shadows in the middle of winter at a locked-up court at the edge of a measly river in New Jersey, not just to play a game, but to test a dream.

I like to think, on the court, yes, there are disputes to be settled, but they are not necessarily about your handle, your J, or your footwork in the post. They are about the position you wish to hold in the world once you walk *away* from the court.

It isn't easy to be just anything in the game of basketball. Certainly, you can be the jock, the ball hog, the thug, the scrub, the shit-talker, or any of the dozens of archetypes the game has produced, but *being* isn't basketball's central directive. Its central directive is *to play.* And the game-play is circumscribed—in time and space, but also from its many rules and one's own physical limitations. The style with which one can play the game—according to (and in spite of) its numerous constraints—figured little in my thinking. For some time, I was willing to trust the authority of the game's rules and proprieties. I was born and raised in a nation that was happy to call my immediate ancestors subjects, but reluctant to call them sons and daughters. An unquestioning heir to such a tradition, I trusted that America rewarded those who pursued happiness within the boundaries of the nation's ordinances—both moral and mundane.

I remember, at nine or ten years old, spending hours trying to learn proper form and rules—shoulders square, knees bent, elbow in, reach into the cookie jar. I shot hundreds of foul shots a week, relentlessly, and was eventually frustrated that no matter how much I followed form, it wouldn't guarantee the shot would go in. It was a long time before I learned about touch. You can be taught rules, but you can't be taught touch, and even if you somehow find touch, it doesn't guarantee you you'll be a good player.

It wasn't until I started playing in an all-Filipino men's league in my late teens, that I got an important lesson about what good players do.

Lenny was a stocky guard who eventually went back to play pro ball in the Philippines, a country obsessed with the sport. The archipelago has its own blood-boiling, even violent rivalries, the most classic being the one between Ateneo and La Salle universities. (I heard a fan from one school pulled out a gun on a fan from the other in the middle of a game.) Every barrio in Laoag, where my mother is from, has access to a public court. When farmers aren't raking their rice from baseline to baseline, drying the grains on the pavement, there's likely a pickup game, league, or youngsters shooting around in their flip-flops.

Like many Filipinos, Lenny had the fever. He was sturdily built, had a mean midrange jump shot and an almost mystical court sense and aware-ness. He was a point guard, but had an uncanny ability to rebound at both ends, definitely the kind of game I wanted to emulate.

We were running practice at a nearby church gym and Lenny and I ended up in the paint together when a shot went up. I knew Lenny would be on it. I had quicker feet, so I got position and just like you're supposed to, squatted on his knee to box him out. As the ball came off the rim, I felt a tug at my wrist and a slight shove at my hip as Lenny knocked me off balance just enough for him to swipe the rebound and get the putback. I kind of mad-dogged him as if to say, "You a dirty motherfucker." He just smiled and said, "Hip pull," before he trotted back on D. I learned that somewhere the rules of basketball are written down, but most of us who play have never seen them, let alone read them. They're passed along on the court; the game itself, the mode of transmission, and no one refutes or makes reference to their original authority.

It took me a long time, maybe until now, to figure this out, and I think most American kids get it very early on, but the standards we're told govern a game are not exactly the ones good players play by. I relied on the naïve assumption that great players were great rule followers; on the contrary, great players are great rule-breakers. Yes, the standards are respectfully accepted, but there is a subtle tug of the wrist that subverts the tradition, with no overseer on the blacktop, save a crew of vaguely powerful ghosts as witness.

I think I was rarely so American as when I stepped onto a basketball court, for it was the site of much of my questioning. It was the site of much of my own evolution, not just from adolescence to manhood, but from faith to disbelief.

Right now, I'm watching a bunch of young dudes run at a public park, just minutes from where I grew up. It's almost twenty-five years since I hopped in the Fiero with Phil, Junji, and Jo, pushed a snow shovel across the cracked court surfaces of The Ledge.

The game still calls me, though not in the middle of the night, and sure as hell not in the middle of winter. A couple of the guys wear cutoff T-shirts from the same high school Lenny went to. The Indian kid is rocking a soccer jersey, running point, the only one getting back on the break. The tall guy on the other team runs the floor well and doesn't seem to miss around the paint. The one kid with his shirt off won't shut up. With ten on the court, there is at least one squad waiting winners.

The game is sloppy as shit, but a couple of guys are flashing the lane, driving the baseline, getting low on D, diving for every loose ball. In my lifetime, the game has hardly changed, and I wonder if America has. I wonder what *they're* playing for. I wonder what their parents have dreamed for them. I wonder what we've got to lose.

SECOND QUARTER

SPINNING IN MY HANDS

MARY LINTON

I DISTINCTLY REMEMBER, CAN STILL FEEL THE AMAZEMENT OF, THE first time. When I was growing, the local school system did not believe competitive sports were good for developing young girls—somehow were bad for our ovaries or, more likely, taught us to be confident and assertive. So most days we trundled along in gym class with some mild games of paddleball, a walk on the balance beam, a run around the track. The school's one concession was a once-per-week after-school session of the Girl's Athletic Association. There I got to play basketball full-court on the very same parquet where the varsity men's team defended the school's honor. We weren't coached and games frequently devolved into wild rushes up and down the court. But it was basketball.

I loved, still love, playing basketball. The family farm didn't have a good place for practice or pickup games. I fastened a backboard and hoop to the top of one of the clothesline poles and did the best I could. The lawn was sloped and lumpy, so I never did learn to dribble well, but I could practice a jump shot. I'd work my way around the horn until it got too dark to see the hoop or find the ball in the garden after an errant shot.

On clear, cold nights I'd shoot by starlight until my mother came to the back door and told me to come to bed. Even in the winter I'd go out at the halftime of my hapless Detroit Pistons' televised games to emulate the soft hands and power moves of Bob Lanier: shoulder down, turn to square shoulders to the basket, elevate, and deliver the ball, top hand flapping like a toilet valve.

During my junior year in high school there were only two teams in GAA. The opposing team had two or three conservative Mennonite girls who played hard and tough in their shin-length skirts and prayer caps. I don't know where they learned to play hoops, but they had an instinct for it and were fast and coordinated. Unlike about half the girls on my team. Emily played guard and could get the ball to Rose, a tall-drink-of-Mennonite-water in the post. They were killing us week after week. We needed to learn some plays to compete at all.

Paula, half-Ojibwa and the chair of the drum section in the senior band, convened a session at her house. We practiced a simple crossing pattern and a pick-and-roll between the center and forward. On our first possession at the next GAA afternoon game, Melody, who had just moved back from Brazil and could swear better in Portuguese than English, brought the ball down, called out an impolite word in Portuguese, and passed the ball in to Paula. Melody and I crossed in front of Paula who faked to Melody, then bounced the ball to me. My hands were small and dry, so the ball was a spinning planet in my right hand. I bounced it once then guided it, in an awkward orbit, to the layup. The ball careened off the backboard and into the hoop! The two spectators erupted into surprised cheers, and we were all so astonished our play had worked that the game actually stopped on the court for a moment. We were giggly, ebullient.

Next possession Melody called a different Brazilian curse. Theresa Ann got knocked on her butt when she set the pick; the collision spun her orange wig that she got after her own Irish red hair fell out from leukemia. Paula rolled and dropped a short jumper through the hoop. We worked those two plays like a couple of draft horses. Our sudden organization into a basketball team gave me space to move, to square and shoot unconsciously. It was religion, and we were saved. In fact we won that afternoon and the next week, too. Unfortunately Emily and Rose learned to box out; our winning streak was short-lived.

I know basketball is not all unconscious body knowledge. You still have to think—you have to see the court, see the flow of the game. When your opponent has the ball, you need to watch their hips so they don't fool you. You need to sift for the right play, the right defense. You need to keep a civil tongue in your head and a respect for all involved. (Sometimes that takes a lot of thought.) You fall down in any of these things and your teammates start barking at you to "get your head in the game!" But a game is usually like breaking in and out of time and not knowing specifically what your muscles have been doing for the last several seconds.

I'm getting up there in years and pickup games are harder to come by in my small town. Luckily I find the same body language when swimming, biking, hiking. Early my body learned the rhythm of one foot swinging past the other, the little butt-wiggle used to balance the bike when it starts to skid on gravel or wallow in sand. My body coordinated all four limbs in the free-style, while my active brain sang cowboy songs and old hymns that were punctuated by equally rhythmic breathing.

Best of all, I find my body knowledge when wading the streams and wetlands where I work. Few things give me as much pleasure as stalking an endangered Blanding's turtle or a red-beaked common moorhen, which is actually rare near my home. It's a small joy just to know that my legs will read the water's currents, or the uncertain bottom, and keep me upright. All of the cells necessary to that task are somewhere in the reptilian part of my brain and don't interfere with the all-encompassing tracking and sudden onslaughts of joy.

For me, poetry is also of the body. I don't mean that poetry is about lust or appetites or even death, although those are all rooted strongly in the body. I mean that the form itself is visceral. I know this, can *feel* it. Poetry's physicality became even more obvious to me when I decided to memorize poetry and found it much easier to do so if I walked at the same time. I often hike around local parks and wild lands while chanting poems out loud, surprising the birds with these other songs.

Poets who write in meter must understand poetry's physicality even more than those of us who write free verse. In my own legs, my own lungs, I can feel Robert Frost striding through a leaf tornado and shouting his surprising poem, "November," about "the waste of nations warring" that begins

> We saw leaves go to glory,
> Then almost migratory
> Go part way down the lane,
> And then to end the story
> Get beaten down and pasted
> In one wild day of rain.

Even free-verse poems have rhythm, although sometimes the flow is interrupted with a bit, or lots, of a stagger. Memorizing Pattiann Rogers's "Geocentric" required a breathless sprinting pace with lines like

> Indecent, self-soiled, bilious
> reek of turnip and toadstool
> decay, dribbling the black oil
> of wilted succulents, the brown
> fester of rotting orchids . . .

Her lines pile as branches on the burn pile during brush cutting. On the other hand, Jane Hirshfield's poetry is often a walking meditation, or languid swim on one of the Great Lakes. An hour of slow backstrokes heading from harbor out to Lake Superior's immensity matches the pace of her poem "Tree":

> It is foolish
> to let a young redwood
> grow next to a house.
>
> Even in this
> One lifetime,
> You will have to choose.

That great calm being,
This clutter of soup pots and books—

Already the first branch-tips brush at the window,
Softly, calmly, immensity taps at your life.

My own poetry staggers freely: a walk in the woods, pulling through brambles while simultaneously birding and picking black raspberries. Rhythm becomes more regular when I write in the language of my family, my home. It is the language I have taken around the horn since I started to jabber, the dialect I use when I square my shoulders to the conversation and release my words with a flapping top hand. It's the body rhythm of the whole tribe—100 percent nature, 100 percent nurture. It's Grandma Edith taking me to harvest sassafras root for tea, my Aunt Ginny frying up bluegills, my cousin Dan telling me how to survive a bar fight, my cousin Sharon secretly cranking up M. C. Hammer on the school's intercom system in the middle of fifth hour. Sometimes it is also the words that come from my unconscious and cause those around me to bark, "Play smart."

The pleasure of hearing the native dialect of a poet is reason enough to drop everything and attend poetry readings. Your body gets a chance to internalize the meter of the poet's voice, learn how the poet deals with the staggers in her or his poems—the line breaks, spaces, gaps.

My body stores the rhythms of June Jordan, Robert Bly, Jane Kenyon, Grace Paley, Frank X Walker, and Naomi Shihab Nye, to name a few. Their words go in my ears and somehow get into my lungs, my bloodstream, my sweat glands. At times I need to learn a poet's voice and body rhythm before I can tell if they are putting up a shot or slapping one down. Often my body leans and moves with them as they read. There ought to be cheerleaders and pep bands at these events.

As I was growing, trying to learn basketball any way I could, I unconsciously developed a standard routine at the foul line. The GAA contests could get unruly and most girls got plenty of chances to practice free throws. I'd plant my feet, wait for the ball from the ref, then bounce it two times, spin it in my left hand, bounce it twice again, spin it, then set for the shot. That pretty silly display, given the usual quality of the games, turned the outside noise down so that my body could take over. Now it's the first thing I do when I get the ball out and head to the driveway hoop.

And I do the same thing when I'm reading an unfinished poem out loud to test the rhythm, the images, the truth of the emotion. Two bounces, then spin a new word in my hand, in my mouth. Two bounces and test the metaphor: should the image here be bologna on rye or heart-leaved arnica blooming in grizzly country? Should the word spinning here have a long or short "a"? Hiking, left hand actually rising to the spin.

For a balmy April week a few years ago I conducted a frog and toad survey for a National Lakeshore. From dusk to late night I drove from swamp to marsh to weedy lake to dune swale, and at each of the twenty stops I sat, listened to, and recorded data on the calling, lusty male amphibians. No one else was out there. It was just the toads, spring peepers, chorus frogs, green frogs, and I.

One beautiful rose-colored dusk I watched a male American woodcock perform his sweetly, melancholy, upward spiral and sweeping freefall, complete with his plaintive nasal *peent,* for a disinterested female until I could take it no longer. In the daytime I walked the dunes and woodlands with a heart open to poetry. If I passed you in my beater Ford Escort, you would have seen me spinning words, left hand rising just inside the open driver's window, right hand on the wheel. A basketball-poet taking two bounces, then spinning and birthing the poems.

I wish I could have seen Lucille Clifton spin up "the wind is eating / the world again. / continents spin / on its vigorous tongue" for her poem "a storm poem." I wish Ted Kooser had driven by my porch on the morning he spun up "and over the next field / a thin flag of starlings billows and snaps" for "november 15," or "The peonies are up, red sprouts / burning in circles like birthday candles . . ." in "Mother." It would be a cherished memory to have watched Ellen Bass lift her hand and decide she liked the spin of "The women in my family / strip the succulent / flesh from broiled chicken / scrape the drumstick clean," when describing the way her female forebears use up love in "Eating the Bones." I would gladly have been knocked flat on my back, lost my Portuguese words and wig, for the pleasure of witnessing any of these poems in the making.

But, of course, I wasn't there. It must be rare for one poet to be there when another poet splits two defenders and makes a left-handed layup, sinks the winning free throw after a hard-fought contest, or sets the pick that frees a sonnet or the sweet sound of assonance or alliteration.

Thankfully I can reach back to my growing years and replay Dave Bing bringing the poem up the floor, see M. L. Carr sink one from the corner, or Dave DeBusschere from the foul line. I could even call up Bob Lanier rebounding and making the one-handed outlet pass to a streaking Chris Ford who pulls up and puts the poem in, all net.

It makes my chest heave just thinking about it.

AGAINST ALL ODDS

LINDA NEMEC FOSTER

M Y FATHER WAS QUITE A SPORTS ENTHUSIAST—ACTUALLY, THE TERM
"sports nut" would be more appropriate. He loved just about all of them—
football, baseball, hockey, golf, even bowling. But the one sport that really
got him revved-up was basketball. He never played the sport and he never
went to see many basketball games, but he would be glued to the television
set whenever a Boston Celtics game was broadcast. He followed their stats
religiously and knew every detail, every nuance, of every player.

Why Boston? Why the Celtics? He was born and raised in Cleveland and
visited Massachusetts only once when he went on a church tour with my
mother to visit the Kennedy compound at Hyannis Port. Maybe that was
it: his idol worship of JFK was responsible for John Joseph Nemec, a Polish-
Catholic from Ohio, morphing into a rabid Celtic fan. But I was wrong.

"Against all odds," my father said once when I asked him why he was so
gung-ho for Boston. "Look at the Celtics' glory years from 1957 to 1969
when they won the NBA championship title eleven out of thirteen times.
It don't get no better than that. Against all odds, they kept doin' it. That's
grace under pressure."

When I think about it, he's right. And two other examples of grace under pressure with regards to the game of basketball come to mind: my husband's pickup team during his second senior year in college and my son's love affair with the Gus Macker Tournament when he was in middle school. My husband's grace came despite his genetics: at 5'7" he never once lost his composure when he had to defend against an opposing player who happened to be 6'5". What a guy, I thought, watching from the sidelines. We started dating seriously that year. and the rest, as they say, is history.

Basketball really can't lay claim to the main impetus for our courtship, however. We had been flirting for years. But his team's name, the infamous Stay Cold Pack, was a definite turn-on. Who cared if a Stroh's cold pack had twelve beers and a basketball team only had five players on the court at any given time? I sure didn't as I watched his lithe body go against the odds time and time again. I can't remember how many games they won and how many games they lost. I just know the Stay Cold Pack became part of my vocabulary, and a year later I married their shortest player.

Our son's story is another definition of grace under pressure—of why people play the game and why they keep playing even when they lose. Since he was nine, Brian played basketball regularly with his buddies from the neighborhood, J. R., Max, Watts, Jeff, and Paul. Even though they didn't always play on the organized school teams, they played a lot of basketball on the playground courts at Lakeside. As soon as the snow melted in the spring and it was slightly warm, they would meet after school and ball it up. Brian even brought our Wet Vac one time to dry off the court so they could play. And that's why the guys fell in love with the Gus Macker Tournament: it was all about playing b-ball in the streets.

Brian and his buds played in the Macker for two summers (1993 and 1994) and won only two games. Let me repeat that: they won only two games in two summers. But that didn't stop them from playing the sport they loved and trying desperately to win the tournament's Toilet Bowl, the trophy given for the best of the worst teams. Every team who lost their first game was taken out of their regular bracket and put into a new bracket, the Toilet Bowl. For some, it was an incentive to lose that first game because the winner of this dubiously named bracket got a trophy, and any kind of trophy was pretty cool.

Especially for these guys who weren't used to winning on the courts. And, after a while, they didn't even care about losing. Only about playing the game. Those long summers of doing nothing but dribbling, passing, shooting, rebounding. Those long summers before the pressures of booze, women, and early death would demand another kind of game and another kind of loss.

As for my own personal experience with the sport, I never got the chance to play basketball except for one lame attempt in gym class my freshman year in high school. After being called on repeatedly for "steps," I was quickly dismissed from the team by the gym teacher. Humiliated (but secretly relieved), I turned my attention to volleyball and learned how to serve and spike with the best of them.

But how does all of this relate to my passion for poetry? I stare at the blank page, the blank screen and imagine the perfect dunk, the nothing-but-net whoosh, the last-second maneuver that heaves the ball from center court for a three-pointer that wins the game. I search for that metaphor, the rhythm, the cadence, the jump ball that starts the very first line. I try to enter the zone of the poem where all words become pure movement and nothing else. I imagine all the improbable things in life that should have never happened but did. My father, rooting for a team he had no business rooting for, and living nearly eighty-nine years to bask in their past glory. My husband, forgetting his height on the basketball court and falling in love with a skinny girl from Cleveland. My son, loving the game so much but loving his friends better. And his mother, against all odds, writing poems (ignoring the fact she never took a creative writing course in college) and living—yes, living to tell the story.

THE BALL GOES IN CLEAN

TODD DAVIS

Growing up in Elkhart, Indiana—factories and cornfields sprouting on acre after acre of flat earth—the only poem I wanted to write was on the basketball court where we played pickup ball. No matter the weather. No matter how hot or how dark or how many mosquitoes howled around our sweaty ears.

Basketball was eternal, infinite, like the stars in the sky, like Connie Hawkins's hops and his ridiculously long arms. I suppose I learned more on the basketball court about what Galway Kinnell claims is the very ground of our making than I ever did reciting poems in English class. The court was a place of action and memory and love, where identity was forged in play after play.

At this point in my life, I wonder how to write about such an obsession without embarrassment. What does it mean to still hunger for a game that possessed you as a teenager with such force that the rest of life seemed peripheral, to discover in your midforties your body giving up on the very thing it desires most?

For so many of us in the state of Indiana, basketball was the only game, the only art that mattered, as magical as Houdini, as beautiful as Picasso. The playground was a painting in which our bodies bent, contorted, then relaxed, stretched, slipping through the maze of other bodies, releasing the ball with just the right spin, the proper angle on the board. It's only in the last few years that I realized this form of art was why I became a poet in the first place, why I'd still rather claim to be a baller than a writer.

In the late 1970s, as Bobby Knight was winning his first national championship at Indiana University, I was falling head over heels in love with what I still believe is the greatest game ever devised. That's the curious thing, of course: it's all made up, contrived, a product of one man's imagination. We call it a "game" because it's supposed to be a diversion, not the all-consuming center of one's attention. Yet once I discovered it, once my passion had been kindled by this "game," it ceased to be mere diversion and became the one art form I've ever claimed to comprehend.

During that fateful, late-nineteenth-century winter in Springfield, Massachusetts, Dr. James Naismith—who was clearly part artist, part physical education instructor—offered up to the world what I would call a verse for the body, a sport that broadcasters have referred to (*over* and *over* again, perhaps to its detriment) as poetry in motion. Needless to say, all the players who ever played the game have added their own lines: some dazzling, some modest, all of them contained by a rectangular court, goals hung ten feet high, ball half the size of the basket's mouth.

I was lucky because Dr. Naismith's legacy was everywhere in my hometown. In driveways, at schoolyards, in church parking lots, down alleys, on the sides of barns, or, in winter, inside barn lofts where baskets were nailed to rafters. The hoops themselves were made out of anything we could find, including milk-crates, the rims of garbage-can lids, even discarded bicycle wheels with the spokes pulled out.

It was the beauty of the jump shot, the gravity-defying throw-down, the threaded-needle of the no-look pass that consumed me, that made of this sport a religion. (After all, isn't the best of religion based upon some aesthetic experience?) And after my hoop-ordained salvation, I couldn't find enough hours in the day to pound the ball on the fading lines of paint, to attempt layup after layup, to drive hard toward the lane, an imaginary defender draped over me like a shadow, only to pull up for a fallaway jump shot or an up-and-under teardrop.

On summer evenings, a choir of players stood courtside and would holler if you broke someone's ankles with a crossover or spun into a reverse between three defenders, their long arms swinging and missing as the ball climbed impossibly high, as it came down clean through the net. No doubt that same choir would sing a mocking hymn of defeat if you had the ball stripped or found your shot thrown twenty feet from the basket, help-side catching you midair with nothing but a feeble prayer and a defender, who, as a matter of course, would shout the liturgy at you, proclaiming, "You better get that shit outta here."

You couldn't go anywhere in Indiana without someone trying to proselytize, evangelize, make you fall down on your knees and cry for the love of basketball. At the barbershop, the church social, during a parent-teacher conference, drinking at the bar, gossiping at the beauty parlor, even sorting bolts at the hardware store could lead to a box score or some story about a kid who couldn't miss, or a team that almost made it to the finals, which in our state was sacred because there were no divisions, every school competing against every other school regardless of their size, regardless of how rich or how poor they were, regardless of the color of their skin.

We understood that the body, the ball, and the court were the only things necessary to write a hoop sestina or a caged villanelle, to contribute something artful to towns that offered less than artful choices for living. It was clear to all of us that our devotion to practicing free throws and the hope of a three-point play could lead to divine moments when we felt like what we did and who we were mattered, that somehow this sport could redeem eight more hours on the factory line for our parents, another dull day for us in our seats at school.

Nobody had much money then, so when someone in the neighborhood got a real hoop, a party would ensue. Game after game until it was so dark there wasn't any use in trying to lift the ball toward the basket. Getting that backboard, that new ball or fresh net, was the reason our dads worked double shifts and our moms asked for overtime on Saturdays, took in wash or cleaned other people's houses.

Games would start early in the morning after we gulped down our Lucky Charms or Frosted Flakes and before the midday heat set in. Whether it was one-on-one, three-on-three, Twenty-one, H-O-R-S-E, Knockout, Around the World, or Tip-down, play washed into play because there wasn't any true conclusion to this sport—only a series of dribbling riffs punctuated by the floating grace of a made shot and occasionally interrupted by a trip to the corner store where we would drink RC and make up a story about some move or blocked shot or crazy dunk we wished we could pull off.

The only thing I remember changing as a kid was the seasons: the way the sidewalks were either bare or rained on or covered by snow or ice. Basketball was a constant regardless of the time of year, so even if you lost a pickup game, ball clunking like a proverbial brick, it didn't matter. There was always the chant of "next," the anxious wait to get chosen by another team for another game played to 15, the work you'd have to do on your own so you could school the guy who had just schooled you.

In the middle of our flyover state, the game was one long and enduring epic, filled with the names of all the players who ever gave their bodies to it. (And take it from someone who's sprained his ankles more times than he'd like to remember, who's had his knee fold over on him like a hen sitting on her egg: Bodies are sacrificed to this sport, and most players past forty walk with arthritic limps of one kind or another.) Yet the beauty of this epic was worth any bodily sacrifice we could imagine at fourteen or fifteen, and the journey seemed never-ending because we were already home, living in basketball nirvana, the best state in the union for the game and its sacred mythology.

We were surrounded by flat fields, by corn and beans. There was no sea to cross, no beast to defeat at the gates, no abandoned lover to return to. Instead our teams' yellow school buses ferried us from town to town in the Kingdom of the Round Sphere, and all of us were vying to be princes in its palatial court, trying to prove ourselves by offering up points and rebounds and assists to the basketball gods we'd heard so much about from our parents and grandparents, who it seemed remembered each sectional, regional, semi-state, and state final ever played.

Our yearning was about the need to rise up for a few seconds, to soar above the hardwood floor or macadam court, all eyes on a single player as he brought the ball around his back, as the defender lurched forward only to miss the steal. We watched the elbow straighten, the wrist snap into the shape of a goose's neck, and the ball sailing like an arrow to find its mark, clean and true.

The reason so many of us got out of bed and climbed the black stairs of the bus was so we could have a chance to play for the school team, and, inevitably, something that was said in class would sink in. I can't remember who first introduced me to the modernist poet William Carlos Williams, but I know it happened in school. What most folks didn't know, however, was that around the same time Williams was uttering his famous dictum for poetry—No ideas but in things!—Hank Luisetti had begun to change the form of the long-practiced two-hand set shot to a more modern-looking and decidedly more effective one-hand jump shot. Luisetti and Williams, who worked at their distinctive art forms long before I was born, irrevocably changed my life and the way I thought about basketball and poetry.

My devotion to "Coach" Williams's notion that ideas should be transported to the reader on the backs of real, concrete objects, the things of the everyday world, and "Coach" Luisetti's admonition to allow the off-hand to drop away at the apex of the jump shot, undoubtedly transformed the basketball poems I've tried to write on blank pages and basketball courts over the years. In the end, there are no "ideas" on the basketball court: only movements, actions and reactions, the physical laws of the universe and the artistic laws of the sport, which we hope will be judiciously enforced by the referees in their stripes. While coaches and players do *think* about the game, studying it, talking about "ideas" that might help them compete, ultimately those "ideas" cannot take to the court and perform the very real acts that are firmly rooted in the material world, in the lift of the elbow, in the curve of the wrist, in the words that open the window on our fleshly existence.

During my college playing days, I was the only English major on the team, and when one of my professors offered up Archibald MacLeish's koan—"A poem should not mean but be"—I began to understand why what I did on the court was just as important, maybe more important to me, than anything I ever did in the classroom. It's awfully easy when you're spending a good portion of your waking hours sitting on your butt, reading novel after novel, poem after poem, essay after essay, to live exclusively in your head, to allow ideas and theory to rule your life. You should never forget how your legs will carry you, how your lungs will fill to meet any need, how your body will respond like a joyful dog when asked to chase after a ball and nine other guys running the court.

I wish more sportswriters would take note of MacLeish. I'm convinced that the wonder of basketball is to be found in its Zen-like nature, in the ten thousand things that comprise it. The fact that we are situated in the present as we move about the court in a yin-yang relation to the other players, continuously transformed from offense to defense, allows me to be present, to stop the chattering voice of my monkey mind and to be fully immersed in my body.

The player who dwells on the meaning of a successful or unsuccessful play—a juke-drive to the basket or a blown defensive assignment—is already lost. The fluid motion of the basketball-present demands a fidelity, a loyalty, and rewards those who practice such a way of seeing with a sense that time has expanded, that it has slowed down so that one can see the play developing even before it comes to fruition.

This is a game of patience, and these days I'm trying to convince my sixteen-year-old son that it isn't about the player who can outsprint everyone, impatient to write the future with layup after layup, but, rather, about the person who accepts this particular moment's demands, at times for speed, at other times for the craft and deception of coming to a near stop, always in balance with one's own body and those bodies that dart like fish in the watercourse of the basketball court.

In the midst of a game there are no replays as on television, no piped-in music to charge a crucial scene with emotion. It's the writers and producers (and, yes, even poets) who after the fact fabricate such moments. Indeed, these sports pundits and their accompanying entourage of camera operators, sound technicians, and editing crews are like poetry critics who toil away at interpretation, who must attempt to delineate the most important line or image, to say where the ballgame and the poem were either won or lost.

And I do not make this comparison disparagingly. I love some of the work these "critics" produce. It's why each year I can't go to bed after the national championship until I've watched "One Shining Moment," an entire NCAA Tournament's worth of hoops stuffed into about four minutes and accompanied by the sweet melodrama of its theme song. I even weep some years for the joy or sorrow of particular players and teams. But having spent so many years around this game, I know during the actual competition, there isn't time or space enough to consider which moment is the most crucial, which shot is the defining point of a game or someone's career.

Growing up, the last thing any kid in my class wanted to be was the next James Whitcomb Riley, who we were told repeatedly represented Indiana's literary finest. If you'd told me I was going to write poems some day, I would have thought you were on some drug-induced trip, in the grips of what my parent's generation called reefer madness. Little Orphan Annie's thudding meter and simple rhyme seemed ridiculous when compared to Lloyd B. Free's wheeling moves to the basket or David Thompson's seemingly never-ending rise toward the hoop. There were no poets, no writers, we knew or wanted to emulate. Our desires matched our parents' and teachers' and coaches' desires: We wanted to be the next Scott May or Kent Benson, to play college ball for Bobby Knight at Alumni Hall in Bloomington and later star for Bobby Leonard and the Pacers at Market Square Arena.

Out of reverence (and, perhaps, with the hopes that such an act might bring favor from some basketball deity), I plastered my walls with posters of the basketball stars. Dr. J, Afro bobbing, arms extended, hand swallowing the ball and circling to the hole. George Gervin, as cool as any glacial flow, the finger-roll of the Iceman ascending over the fingertips of Artis Gilmore. Paul Westphal shooting with either hand, somehow slipping between two defenders for a midrange jumper, scoring yet another 30-point game. Wes Unseld clearing space to pluck rebound after rebound from the glass, and Elvin Hayes catching the ball at midpost, spinning in the air to nail a drifting jumper as the Washington Bullets won the NBA championship during my eighth-grade year.

I would watch games like a PhD candidate studying for exams. At the playground. At the high school gym. If I was lucky, on one of the three stations our television antenna might lasso. I scrutinized the movement of feet, feint of shoulder, the placement of hands or forearm on an opponent's back or midsection. I made note of the ways the lines ran the length of the court, the manner by which they controlled the patterns and spacing of the players.

Stephen Dunn contends that "if basketball offers you the possibility of transcendence, it more regularly offers you a sense of your limitations." But the splendor of basketball, as in poetry, is that each player, each writer, brings something unique, altogether different, to the form, in spite of or because of his or her limitations. Like jazz or hip-hop, basketball, at its best, is about improvisation, about inventing new ways to get by your defender, to take the ball to the rack or hit a teammate at the goal.

No matter how many times you've run the pick-and-roll, no matter how complete you think your understanding of the give-and-go, if you are alive and present to that next moment, you realize it isn't the same play, that each time there is something to be reborn or revived out of the repetition.

Science generalizes, asking us to ignore the subtle differences between two members of the same species in order to create taxonomies of knowledge. Coaches and critics follow the same paradigm when introducing a new play or judging a new poem, trying to define a particular defense or fit a poet into a particular school. Yet just as flowers and trees of the same genus will surprise you by their capriciousness, no play in basketball can ever be run exactly the same way twice, and no poem worth rereading will be purely imitative.

Thankfully, there are endless variables in poetry, basketball, and science. What else would we expect from life's miracles? And because of such wide-ranging unpredictability each moment shines with mystery. This is the sweet sap of wonder, the rejuvenation we turn to art and sport to experience again and again. As Gerard Manley Hopkins declaims, "for all this, nature is never spent; / There lives the dearest freshness deep down things." Perhaps, if Hopkins had lived to witness Steve Nash dribbling off a pick from Amare Stoudemire, seeing the big man reverse-pivot to the basket, pass thrown perfectly to the front of the rim, the flush of the ball, he would have confessed that this was the "freshness" of which he spoke, the sprung rhythm in the flesh.

At forty-six, my job as a poet has forced me to leave Indiana. My body has broken down a bit, the results of too many trips up and down the court and their attendant injuries. Yet I still can't bring myself to give up the game. More and more, it's the jump shot that helps me compete against younger players. But every so often I sneak by someone using a rocker step, or what little quickness I have left, and I find myself taking off on the right side of the basket, defying age and gravity, only inches from the floor where it used to be feet, scooping the ball from my waist over my right shoulder, seeing a reverse layup go in or spotting an open teammate under the basket.

I suppose the challenge of age, of waking each morning, is to flee those desperate lives Thoreau chided so many for falling into. While I didn't learn all that much about poetry growing up in Indiana, I did receive a valuable lesson about the artfulness of living. Most of the people I knew worked in factories making RVs or car parts for Detroit, detailing converted vans or putting One-a-Day vitamins in bottles for Miles Laboratories. Despite the fact that the line was a deadening, repetitive job, these folks didn't lose sight of the human need for rhythm and dance, for the play of language in nicknames and taunts. They're the choir that still sings in my head when I pick up a ball, why I still want to hear one more twine of the net as the ball goes in clean.

Put simply: they're the only reason I ever tried to write a poem in the first place, whether it's on the court or on the page.

HARD

PETER SEARS

I HANG AT THE HIGH SCHOOL BIKE STANDS AND LOCK MY BIKE AND then, pretending not to like my spot, unlock my bike and move it to another spot and lock it up again. I do this a couple of more times to come to homeroom with her already in her seat up front so that I can pretty much stare at her the whole homeroom period without anyone noticing. My friends, if they find out, will work me over. So I am careful sneaking good looks at her, like I'm putting a cape over her and drawing her to me, saying things to her that I can't even hear.

After homeroom, I probably won't see her again until after lunch. That's okay. Lunch is dicey because I sit with my friends, who gawk around, crack dirty jokes, and guffaw. So that means I don't see her until Latin, sixth period. She's terrible at Latin. When she is asked to translate, I just die. She doesn't know anything. I doubt she cracks a book. I love Latin. I love her. If only I could save her, swoop her up in my arms and carry her down the hall to, like, shop or study hall, or maybe right out to the ball fields, murmuring Latin love words. That way she wouldn't understand a word and would have to ask me what I'm saying. I'd just smile. But maybe I can't carry her that far, she is bigger than I am.

In Latin, when I am called on, I try not to speak too enthusiastically. I don't want everyone thinking I am doing it for her. I am doing it for her. I do everything for her. Have you heard of the ablative absolute? Well, that's what the Latin teacher asked her about. She sat there. I wanted to stand up and shout, Ask somebody who knows! Like me! Ask me! But I cowered there, for her, for me, for everyone crushed by an ablative absolute. We don't even have the ablative case in English. The teacher is just mean.

I should be grateful, I guess, I am not in any of her other classes. English class could be worse because when they didn't have enough copies of *The Merchant of Venice,* they switched to *Romeo and Juliet.* What if I had to read Romeo when she read Juliet? I'd commit suicide. Well, pretty close. What if someone else got to read Romeo when she read Juliet? I'd hate him, I'd challenge him to a duel and he would probably say, "You're crazy," and my friends would laugh their asses off. I'd like to ask Romeo about his baggy pants and what about dancing with Juliet, pressing her to him?

What I'd really like is to get taller. Coach is asking me about it. We have this play where I set a screen for the other guard, but I'm so short the guy guarding me can just reach over me and block the guy's shot. So I don't get to go in for that screen play anymore. I'm sent in now only to foul guys, to keep our starting players from fouling out. The ref likes to yank my jersey up to see my number and holler it out. He says he'll call a technical foul on our team if I can't keep it tucked in. I don't believe him, he can't be that mean, but coach believes him. Coach likes to say, "I ask you to take one foul, not two," and look around as if he just made it up.

I would much rather keep my jersey tucked in anyway because, when it hangs down over my shorts, it looks like I only have a shirt on. That's what my friends say, laughing their asses off as usual. The cheerleaders look away, embarrassed for me. I could die. But I can get up and down the court faster than anyone. They call me Butterfly. They call me Speeding Bullet. They call me Winger. I dribble too hard, the ball comes up too high. I outrun the ball, but one thing about playing, I don't worry about what my crazy body is doing.

The problem is I don't get into the game very often—maybe every third game—and just long enough to foul some guy, who looks at me as if I'm a jerk. So most of the time I am sitting on the bench. When coach calls your name to go in the game, he leans over and shouts it down the bench to paralyze you. It paralyzes me. I have to stand up. What I do if I have been thinking of her and getting a little crazy is to lean over and rush up along the bench to the coach and lean down on one knee to get instructions—you know, like which guy to foul—and then I slide over to the scorer's table, check in, lean down on one knee and pray. I don't look down.

If she were at the game, I wouldn't care if I didn't play a second. There are always the warm-up drills, she'd see me. I could wave. I wouldn't do that, though. And if I did get to play, I'd play much better with her cheering. I could whisper to her later that she had inspired me. She probably wouldn't believe me, but I could smell her breath and her hair and try to store it in my memory.

Cheerleading tryouts are coming up. I hope she tries out. I know she would make it, she's so pretty. But maybe not. A friend of hers told me that she is not trying out because she thinks cheerleading is dumb—where is her school spirit?—and she doesn't want to go to all those away games, and she can't jump, and she doesn't want to learn the dumb cheers. Heck, you learn them by hearing them all the time. She'd be a gorgeous cheerleader. I can see her on their bench, that skirt, that sweater, those little white sneakers. Makes me dizzy.

I dream of her waiting for me after practice and, sure, walking home together. I would probably be aching big time pretty much the whole way and trying not to show it, you know, just talking and walking slowly, carrying her books and not looking down.

Once I speak to her, that's it. She will know I like her and tell her friends, and then everyone will know. I might as well carry a sign around, but I sure would be proud to be her boyfriend. I would hate people asking me questions about us, though. I'd want to say that I'd like to talk with her about it first. Then they might think I wasn't much of a guy.

What I'd really like is to hang around and talk with her as if we were just hanging around, but I don't know how to do that. I mean, what do you say when you don't have anything to say? Some guys are good at that. They talk to girls a lot, the popular guys. My life isn't like that. I go to class, I have my friends, I go to practice, I do my homework, and I take care of my bike. Sometimes, I'm called to the principal's office and help with some sorting. The secretaries are nice to me. I don't know much of anything else. I know what happens, though, when I think of her. It hurts.

IN PRAISE OF BAD BOYS AND
THE EVOLUTIONARY LEAP

THERESE BECKER

TODAY, AS I DRIVE THROUGH MY SUBURB ON MY WAY TO THE MARKET, I notice how almost every home has a basketball net either above the garage or adjacent to the driveway. I smile as I think how it's just one more change in the landscape we now take for granted. I remember the Detroit neighborhood where I grew up where the only kids who had a basketball net lived in the wealthy neighborhoods. The kids in my neighborhood, on the other hand, had to make do with kick-the-can, tag, climbing trees and building forts out of nothing, scaling up and down the huge billboards along the highway, and our favorite: playing baseball in the street—running bases, batter up in between as the traffic allowed.

Street baseball served me well as it gave me enough experience to eventually become part of St. Juliana's grade-school team that would capture the city championship. I can still remember fervently promising the Blessed Mother during the final game that if she would help us win, I would say a rosary every day for the rest of my life, and I was only in the eighth grade.

And then we won. Lesson learned: never make a promise you are unlikely to keep.

After a year of rosaries, exhausted and guilty I went into the confessional and begged a priest to please release me from this promise. Did he think I had paid enough so far for our victory? I'm sure I made his day as he quickly absolved me, and I walked out light as a feather into a world where "Hail Mary" evolved into the pass the guys made on the football field, and to where I looked forward to those other passes that boys were expected to make. Bad boys, in particular, became the newest sport we Catholic girls had to learn how to play.

This was the fifties where the all-girl and all-boy Catholic high school reigned supreme—perhaps the church thought it would lead us all to embrace celibacy, the nunnery, and the priesthood? Distance, however, could not stop the hormones from swirling, and as the old cliché says: makes the heart grow fonder. Separation, as I recall, only led many of us to become "boy crazy" and forever in search of the forbidden fruits which, of course, were most present at the all-boy school's sporting events.

I ended up attending Dominican High School with the rest of my girl-friends, one of the most prominent all-girl schools where we dressed like clones in our loose, blue uniforms, and really hated the nylons we were required to wear under our bobby sox. But that wasn't the worst of it—in gym class we had to wear the most god-awful, putrid yellow uniforms that still make me shudder.

There were only two sports available to us then: field hockey, where you knew if you made the team, you would have to appear in public wearing what looked like your grandma's used underwear, and no guy who spotted you would ever again think of you as female from that point on; and basketball—which I thought would at least keep me indoors and hopefully hidden away from the male observer. Plus, I had all of my height by fifth grade, and could still hear the family's words ringing in my ears: wow, you're going to be a great basketball player! So I took the leap, but sadly it didn't become a love affair like baseball had been; it became, instead, one of the biggest disappointments in sports that I've ever experienced.

It seems the world had not yet shaken the image of the frail female that it had to protect from the rough-and-tumble action enjoyed by the boys when they played basketball. After all, we were girls, and we might get hurt moving around out there on the court, and history said we could only do safe things, like carrying a child within us for nine months, and then delivering it without anesthetics (after a hard day's work in the field) with (if we were lucky) the assistance of a neighbor and some hot water.

The rules in 1954 were that a girl could only dribble the basketball twice, and then she had to pass it on to a teammate. It felt like your body had a continual and aggravating case of hiccups. Kick-the-can had more fun and fluidity in it than this joke that they dared to call basketball. While the gunnysack gym-suit said that our bodies were something to be concealed, feared, dangerous even, this game of beauty and grace, joy and excitement was revised and handed over to the girls like a stillborn facsimile. It eventually became a metaphor for me for the myriad limits still in place on women in the fifties. Needless to say, I only lasted on the team for a few weeks. Lesson learned: never settle for second best, or shortchange yourself just because you happened to have been born with a vagina.

In time my husband and I and our three children moved out into what my mother dubbed: No Man's Land. We loved the "boonies" for many reasons, and not the least of which was living only a few minutes away from the Palace of Auburn Hills: home of Motown's legendary basketball team, the Detroit Pistons, aka the Bad Boys.

When they were at their peak and won back-to-back championships in 1989 and 1990, some of the greatest sport's memories I now have with my husband happened in the nosebleed section where, once the action started, we rarely sat down, and cheered and sang till our throats became raw. Even today, though cancer took him from us over six years ago, every time I drive by the Palace, I shout out a hello to him and smile as he will forever remain the baddest boy I've ever known.

When there wasn't a home game, we were glued to the TV no matter what occasion we were at. One of my writer friends, who had never been swept up by a sport's love affair, is perplexed to this day at the fervor with which I followed the Bad Boys. She would wonder aloud how anyone could love poetry and the Bad Boys in the same lifetime. She no longer had a slot that I could neatly fit into, and I'm sure that was a small part of why it all made me feel so good. But the other part (which you either felt or you didn't) was that I had finally found poetry in the game of basketball as I watched those Boys play their hearts out on the court. Why, they even wore black jerseys when they practiced, complete with a skull and cross-bones logo on it. Now that was a gym uniform I could have worn with great pride.

Game after game, in my imagination I sailed across that court with them, slam-dunked, and hit the net from center court inside my mind's eye. And I loved the delicious nicknames some of them were given for their special abilities, like Dennis Rodman, the Worm; John Salley, Spider; Vinnie Johnson, the Microwave, and John Edwards, the Buddha. Now how could they have a Buddha on their team if they were really bad boys? But then again, how could they not?

Rick Mahorn and Bill Laimbeer became the most hated Boys of all because they were such an unstoppable duo, and even though we chanted "Bad Boys," we knew in our hearts that what began as an announcer's tag had simply run away with itself—the way gossip tends to create a new life of its own. Poor Laimbeer would have fouls called on him at times for what seemed simply like taking a deep breath—at least to his fans. The joke among those who loved him was that after a foul was called on Laimbeer, the referee to his embarrassment would notice that Laimbeer was still on the bench. The more the referees, other teams, and the media threw darts at the Bad Boys, the more the fans loved them and defended them. Laimbeer eventually became a four-time all-star. And today I can see how—due to the rivalry that developed during those years between Isiah Thomas, our captain, and Michael Jordan—it took me many years to open up to the obvious legendary gifts for the game that Jordan was blessed with.

We were all caught up in the criticism of the "other," and not only did it cloud my view, but I'm sure it blocked others from seeing each player as an individual with a history behind him. For instance, Dennis Rodman never played high school basketball, but he was still picked in the 1986 NBA draft. He also won two Defensive Player of the Year awards and several rebounding titles, despite a very difficult childhood to overcome. All that most people see, even to this day, is his dyed blond hair and the bad outfits he wore off the court.

The Bad Boys established in 1989 one of the best records in NBA history. Detroit will never forget Johnson's game-winning shot in game 5 of the 1990 NBA Finals, with only seven seconds to go: final score, Detroit 92; Portland, 90. And one of my sons will never forget the night he played pool all night with Rodman at a local bar. He still talks about what a nice, humble guy that Bad Boy really was. And in 2002, the baddest of the boys, Bill Laimbeer, would become the coach of the Detroit Shock, one of the first professional women's basketball teams in the WNBA. He would boldly predict that they would win the championship the following year, and they did. Lesson learned: Don't judge anyone by what someone else says about them. Stand back and enjoy (perhaps be part of) their evolution. Be aware that you never fully know the history that brings them to where they now are. Titles can be deceiving.

Being a poet in love, it was inevitable that eventually I would take that love and fascination to the page and write a basketball poem. The trigger for the poem was when Magic Johnson, during a funny skit at halftime, was asked what basketball might be like in the year 2020. He answered: "People will be able to fly. Everybody will be above the rim." I jumped up off of the sofa and wrote it down because I could feel the poem within. The poem that I wrote was later published in *Full Court: A Literary Anthology of Basketball.* When the editor called to accept the poem, he said: I like your vision and I hope it comes true. You never know what the poem is going to tell you until it does, and this one told me that we could win the game everyone thought was impossible to win. The poem was written before movies like *What the Bleep* appeared on the horizon, so obviously Magic Johnson was also tuning into "something" moving in the spheres out there, and readying us for the next evolutionary leap.

Quantum physics now tells us that the observer shapes the world that exists before them. Did the hope for change in all of those unhappy girls who were forced to play the stunted version of basketball eventually free up the game to embrace all that they were really capable of? Did this collective, evolving vision of what we wanted to be available for our own girls now bring me to these bleachers where I was able to first watch my daughter play like a gazelle on the court, and next watch my granddaughters do the same?

Just a few years ago most people in the United States couldn't believe that they would ever see a black man in the White House. But as President Obama began to see himself there, we too were caught up in a vision that has forever shifted our reality as a country. Now, he moves with the finesse he used to move with on a basketball court across the largest and most powerful court in the world.

In July 2008, President Obama, in a ceremony at the White House honoring the Detroit Shock, who won three WNBA championships in six years, acknowledged how grateful he was as a father for women's teams such as this that show his daughters what they can aspire to accomplish in the world of professional sports if they so choose. The WNBA had been around for twelve years, and as a result he said that his daughters have never known a time when this vision didn't exist for them.

I'm sure there are many more lessons waiting for me inside the world of sports since all of my grandchildren continue to embrace the multitude of opportunities now open to both boys and girls. This world is an expanding classroom that continues to teach me, and so I try to pay attention, and listen as deeply as I am capable in the moments left to me on the planet.

Who could have imagined, so many years ago, that those bad gym uniforms and a team full of Bad Boys would eventually help to expand my consciousness? It comforts and challenges me that I am a part of all I observe, and that I am moving each moment with everyone across the world's court—leaping, crying, walking into walls, falling, laughing, but most of all enjoying a wonderful evolutionary leap into the realm of anything's possible.

Lesson learned: the game is never really over. In fact, it's always just beginning.

WHY I WROTE THE "MAGIC" JOHNSON POEM

QUINCY TROUPE

As a young man, I was a basketball player, a point guard, who was also the coach out on the floor. Point guards are good passers, dribblers, and they run the offense. I could pass and dribble, and I was a scorer, too. I wanted to win, to be a champion, and I always played on championship teams. I learned that if I played the game unselfishly, passed to teammates when they were open, everyone would be happy and we would play better as a team. And we did. We played well together because we were all unselfish players. We won because we played together, passed the ball to whoever was open. Those were the keys to winning.

When I first saw "Magic" Johnson play, he was a senior in high school. I watched him play in an all-star game. He scored a lot of points, and he also passed the ball a lot to teammates who were open. So he got many assists. He was a good rebounder, too. That impressed me. His team won. It was very important to me that Magic's team won, because for me he personified the ideal team player. After high school, I watched him during his college career. His Michigan State team won the 1979 national championship during his sophomore year, beating the great Larry Bird's Indiana State team in the finals.

Magic turned professional at the end of his sophomore year of college and became Rookie-of-the-Year in his first professional season. He also led the Los Angeles Lakers to the 1980 NBA Championship in his rookie season, beating the Philadelphia 76ers, led by the legendary Julius "Dr. J" Erving in the Championship game. In the title game Magic scored 43 points, hauled in 15 rebounds, dished out 7 assists and had 3 steals. In this game, Magic played point guard, forward, and center, substituting for the great Kareem Abdul-Jabbar, who had injured his ankle. This game made Magic a legend in his first year playing in the NBA. It was an unforgettable beginning to what turned out to be a Hall of Fame career.

Magic was a very tall point guard, 6 feet 9 inches, while others who played this position were less than 6 feet 4 inches. Being this tall allowed Magic to look over his shorter opponents and see the whole court. This was a huge advantage, and Magic always used it. Magic was also agile and quick. He could pass better than anyone else during his era—and remains one of the greatest passers of all time. He was a skillful dribbler as well. He played a short man's game with a tall man's body. He was beautiful to watch on the court. He was a great dancer and a magician: I loved to watch him play because he was literally "poetry in motion."

I'd always wanted to write a poem about a basketball player. I'd tried many times unsuccessfully. Now Magic inspired me to write the poem I'd always wanted to write. One day in 1985, when I was living in New York City, I sat down and started writing the poem. I felt in order to write a successful poem about basketball, the words and language in the poem had to capture the speed of the game: also, the images employed in the poem had to mirror and echo those of the game. The art of free-verse poetry is perfect for capturing something as lyrical, fast, dexterous, athletic, and free-flowing as a basketball game. Free-verse poetry is also perfect for capturing the moves of great players participating in one of the most balletic—if not *the* most balletic—of sporting games. To excel in the upper echelon of the sport, especially playing in the guard or forward positions, one must possess the skills of a great dancer. Usually, the sense of speed, agility, and magic of great basketball players can be best captured by music—jazz or the rhythms of rap. It can also be captured in the words and language of free-flowing poetry.

When I first began to write poetry in the early 1960s, I was in the army, living in France and playing basketball both on an army team and a French team. A knee injury ended my days as a player, and while I was recuperating from my injury, I started writing poetry. At first, it was tough sledding because I didn't know the first thing about metaphor, similes, meter, forms, or any kind of poetic structure (all of which I later taught myself). When I returned to the United States in the spring of 1963, I began reading all the poetry I could lay my hands on. I grew to admire the poetry of Pablo Neruda, Langston Hughes, T. S. Eliot, and others. My poetic voice matured after I moved to Los Angeles during the summer of 1963, specifically after I joined the Watts Writers Workshop in early 1966. I soon discovered my natural poetic breath. The length of the line I wrote was closer to a long twelve-syllable hexameter line—and many times even longer than that— than it was to a natural American ten-syllable, iambic line. Perhaps this was the influence of Pablo Neruda's poetry on my work—immense at the time—and the fact that I was living in Los Angeles, a sprawling city of cars, freeways, trees, mountains, the Pacific Ocean, and very few people walking the streets and very little "public life"—as I discovered later, when I moved to New York City—during these years.

Without a doubt all of the above were influences on my writing a longer, more melodic, yet rhythmically poetic line influenced by jazz, sermons, the blues, rock and roll, and African American speech patterns. At the same time I came under the influence of such American poets as LeRoi Jones (later known as Amiri Baraka), Robert Hayden, Allen Ginsberg, Ed Dorn, and Bob Kaufman. My poetry was also affected by the Peruvian poet César Vallejo; the Columbian novelist Gabriel García Márquez; the Mexican novelist Juan Rulfo; the Madagascan poet Jean-Joseph Rabearivello; the poet Aimé Césaire from Martinique; and Léon Damas from French Guyana.

All of these influences can be seen in my poems from this period, especially in many of the lines from the poem "Ode to John Coltrane," written on the occasion of the saxophonist's death in 1967. Notable throughout this long poem are the influences of Neruda, Dylan Thomas, and the rhythms of jazz, in the use of repetition and sprung rhythms.

In contrast, when I moved to New York City, Manhattan to be exact, in 1971, the length of my poetic line began to change. At first my poetry was a mixture of long, medium, and short lines, and reflective of the culture of a bustling, pedestrian city, filled with the "public life" of people everywhere, and at all hours of the day and night. The sound of traffic—buses, cars, trucks, horns honking—people's voices, dogs barking, the voices of street vendors, music blaring from churches on Sundays, musicians playing jazz, Latin, and classical music everywhere in the streets. Rap music was beginning then, accompanied by young men doing incredible break-dancing, spinning on their heads on cardboard spread over the ground on street corners, their legs and feet twirling in the air. They even practiced their art on subways, commuter trains, and on ferryboats crossing over to Staten Island. The underground sounds in the subway fascinated me: the sound of trains, their wheels clicking and licking the tracks, police sirens and fire engines wailing on their way to extinguish fires, street theater, people arguing, gunshots, screams in the night, cats screeching, a multiplicity of quixotic noises rising and swelling and punctuating the life of that dynamic city.

By 1985, when I wrote the poem "For Magic," I was amid all these rhythms and sounds of New York City. Increasingly my poetic lines had been getting shorter, mirroring the culture in which I was now ensconced: quick, shifting rhythms, myriad wordplays, quixotic sounds popping up from out of nowhere, a multicultural brew of languages sluicing through the air everywhere in Manhattan. It was magical. The city seemed to change every day in 1985. All of this had a definite and profound influence on "For Magic," because in composing this poem, I reached the apex of an urban, lightning-quick linguistic style I had been moving toward ever since I'd arrived in New York City. After "For Magic," I wrote other poems that were influenced by life in New York, though they never quite equaled what I was able to achieve in the poem for the "Magic man."

In "For Magic," I used colorful words and descriptions to capture Magic Johnson's amazing moves on the court. I employed his stop-and-go, herky-jerky style of play as the rhythmic foundation for the poem. In other words, the poem's rhythm had to "pop" into the eyes and ears of the reader and listener, as the poem was read out loud. Plus the tempo and pace of the language of the poem had to be quick, with rapid shifting phrases, like rhythms in rap, or in an improvisational jazz solo, simulating those of a basketball game. Also, the line breaks in the poem had to move in this same manner. For example, I indented the seventh line of the poem,

cause you wiped glass backboards

so it could stand apart from the rest of the text. I wanted it to be a long, lean line, echoing Magic Johnson's height and physicality at the time. But I enjambed the end of the line—"so clean"—down on the next line, to set up the "herk & jerk" (which starts the third line at the top of the poem), feeling I wanted to run through the poem.

I employed the same technique throughout the poem for the same effect, indenting the following lines: ("a new-style fusion of shake & bake" and enjambing "energy" onto the next line: Indenting "stop & go dribble," which followed "off the high yoyo patter": "his skyhook pops the cords," which proceeded "to kareem cutting through the lane"; and "you double-pump through human trees," and then I indented "hang in place" and enjambed "slip" to the next line, which is followed by "the ball into your left hand." There are other examples like this when the line "& we cheer with you, rejoice with you," is followed by the indented stand-alone line, "for this quicksilver, quicksilver," which is followed by the enjambed "quicksilver moment of fame" on the next line. The last example of this technique in the poem is in the fifth line from the bottom, "hang in place," which is followed by the indented line, "& put it all up in the sucker's face, magic Johnson," which is followed by the enjambed lines: "& deal the roundball like the juju man that you am / like the sho-nuff shaman that you am, 'magic,' / like the sho-nuff spaceman you am."

There are other places throughout this poem where I employ herky-jerky rhythms, shifting patterns of speech and neologic words and phrases like "everwhichaway," "juked & shook," "shake & glide & ride up in space," "hammer home a clothes-lining deuce off glass," "hoodoo gem / off the spin & stick it in sweet, popping nets clean / from twenty feet, right side," "slide the dribble behind your back, ease it deftly / between your bony stork legs, head bobbing everwhichaway," "off the high yoyo patter / stop & go dribble / you thread a needle-rope pass sweet home," "your legs scissoring space / like a swimmer's yoyoing motion in deep water," or "alley-oop dunkathon magician passes."

These are the primary techniques I used throughout the Magic Johnson poem, trying to create an effective work. I wanted to employ conscious elements of surprise and improvisation—as in the best work in jazz and rap. Also I hoped to mirror not only the greatness and originality of one player—Magic Johnson—but also the greatness, speed, creativity, and majesty of basketball itself, especially when it is played at a high, creative, and competitive level.

I wrote and rewrote "For Magic" over fifteen times, until I finally felt I had it right. It was hard work, but I was happy with the finished poem. The response from audiences of all ages and backgrounds, throughout the world, wherever and whenever I've read this poem, elicits enthusiastic responses, and it never ceases to amaze me. I hope you like it, too.

HALFTIME

THE ART OF THE CHEER

DEBRA MARQUART

Poetry was no longer a strange and irrelevant loveliness in a chaotic world;
it was a necessary and consummate flowering on the great tree of life; it was
the immanent purpose of the universe made vocal.

—*THE ORPHIC VOICE*, ELIZABETH SEWELL

1.

The afternoon I bought my first record, "Red Rubber Ball" by the Cyrkle,
I went to my best friend Jovita Becker's house. She plucked the single from
the sleeve and dropped it onto her turntable with a crunch of the needle
as the sound of the Farfisa organ rang out, and we danced the Pony on the
bouncy, wood floor of her upstairs bedroom. I went to her house often, late
afternoons, after Catholic school, while her parents were still at work at their
grocery store.

It was the first metaphor I understood to be a metaphor (*The rollercoaster ride we took is nearly at an end*), and perhaps the first simile (*The morning sun is rising like a red rubber ball*), because we talked about such things, the poetry of song lyrics, just as we wore each other's clothes and secretly applied her older sister's makeup on each other's eyes and cheeks and lips, trying out our future faces.

2.

And in Jovita's bedroom, where we went to get away from her four pesky younger brothers, we made up moves and cheers to accompany pivotal moments in imaginary games to come: *Push 'em* **back**, *push 'em* **back**, *push 'em* **waay back** and **Let's go, let's go, L-E-T-S-G-O.** Our hands clapping, our feet stomping as we released our cheers, our vowels and consonants like desire into the world.

And she was always better at it than me, getting the body's motions to mirror the meaning of the words, all of which she made up, and which I learned from her and mimicked so that the cheer's effect would be doubled in the world.

This was 1966, years before Title IX would reach us. We were tiny beings anyway, ten-year-old girls, our skinny bodies preparing to take our place on the sidelines, preparing to raise our voices in meaningful, structured ways, all in an attempt to embolden the giants among us.

3.

The game of basketball is a closed and finite experiment, designed to test the mettle and training, the natural talents and improvisational skills of its participants. The confines of the game's structure create the effect of heightened drama, because, unlike life, every moment of a basketball game reminds us that something is at stake.

The game unfolds with cold precision, in preset increments of time, the passage of which ticks away in minutes and seconds on a wall display, and whose expiration is announced by horns and buzzers. In basketball, there can be no mystery about where the time has gone; yet, it often slips away inexplicably.

The playing court, too, is defined and preset: a long rectangle of dark floor marks indicating in-bounds, out-of-bounds, front- and backcourt, the free-throw line, the ten-second line, the top of the key—all agreed-upon spaces in which certain things may or may not occur, but places in which invariably many wrong and unfortunate things do occur. Referees dressed in black-and-white striped shirts, to differentiate them from the players, are present on the floor among the players with their whistles to point out, monitor, and officiate the infractions.

The game's impeccable intentions stand in high relief to the foibles of humans: the fumbling inaccuracies, the missteps and double dribbles, the winded back-and-forth rushes of sweaty bodies, the wild passes.

In this small interpretative space, where time slips away, where rules are broken and penalties incurred, a few humans manage to structure moments that coordinate the mastery of eye and hand, breath and foot, that makes basketball unfold like poetry. And it is here, I would suggest, where cheers, artfully enough designed, might also enter the game's calculus and influence outcomes in infinitesimal ways.

4.

My ex-husband told me about the years when he was a young boy, praying in his upstairs bedroom in Rapid City, South Dakota, praying in the bathroom on the toilet, praying in the shower, praying before he went to bed, for the St. Louis Hawks, the Minneapolis Lakers, the Philadelphia 76ers, praying for anyone to beat the Celtics.

Then one day he had this thought—Was some other boy, possibly in New England, praying more fervently in the bathroom, on the toilet, in the shower, praying in bed each day of each year for the Celtics? And weren't there more of such boys in New England than the unpopulated West? So he wondered, Do the prayers of opposing fans cancel each other out and does one team prosper in the imbalance?

Which caused him to puzzle out if God had a team, and, if so, was he Catholic? Or did God watch over the conflagrations of humans like a dispassionate Zeus, while Athena, Apollo, and Artemis interfered with the outcomes of our mortal play?

5.

When it comes up, because it always seems to come up, what we did back in high school, I'll admit I was a cheerleader. In a small town, everyone has to be at least five things—school newspaper editor, choir, 4-H, drama club, cheerleader—in order for the town to function like a proper town. It could have been worse. Braddock, a smaller town thirty miles away, had only one boy in a senior class with eight girls. Imagine how stressful homecoming was for him. Imagine his prom.

We were growing up in Napoleon, North Dakota, a town of short, fierce people named after a short, fierce emperor. At 5'4", I was a female giant in my tribe. Sometimes, at family gatherings, the grandparents would point at me with pride and say, "Look at her long legs."

We were the Imperials, rolling from town to town in my Uncle Ben's school bus in our royal blue and white uniforms. With our short limbs and low centers of gravity, we were born grapplers (North Dakota Class B High School Wrestling Champions: 1975, 1980, 1981, 1982, 1989, 1990, 1997, 2002, 2003, 2004, 2005, 2006, 2007). Yet, I chose to try out for the basketball cheering squad, which reveals my natural instinct to root for the underdog and prefigures my lifelong weakness for the Minnesota Vikings and the New York Knicks.

6.

Into the taut spatial and temporal construct of a basketball game, adversaries must step with only this one round ball to share and fight over among ten players, five people per team. Off the court, they may be friends or admirers, lovers or coworkers, sisters or brothers, but here on the court, everything becomes Either-Or—teammate or opponent, offense or defense—switching back and forth throughout the game, in infinite varieties and configurations.

Above all this, suspended at a lofty height, is the game's other plane, the backboards, the orange rims, and the empty floating nets of the two baskets at either end, to be scored upon or defended. Two empty nets, but only one ball.

The purity of their emptiness drives the action, causing players to pass, to run, to block, to steal, to fumble, to foul, all driven by the urge to fill the opponent's void with the ball in your possession, however momentarily, to feel the swish that will result in a score that will finally count for something.

7.

Those afternoons at Jovita's house, before we were old enough to be cheerleaders, we practiced the high jump, the splits, the hand motions, the sequence of hand claps. We mastered the cartwheel, the back and front flips. We became athletes of cheering.

Our first utterances, the sounds we made in grade school—whispers behind cupped hands, gum pops, sighs, gasps, laughs—grew more organized and filled with intention as we matured. Our sounds made their way to talk, to chatter, to songs; made their way to bad rhymes, then bad poems written in wide-ruled notebooks in sprawls of pink and green ink about bad boys, about boys who didn't notice, about boys who had the moves. *Ronnie, Ronnie, he's our man. If he can't do it, no one can.*

At last, finally, we were selected, given license, to yell, to jump, to scream along the sidelines. We were put in charge of pep; we were given a rally. People got out of fifth period and were required to file onto the bleachers and listen to us as we jumped and shouted about the importance of pep until the whole student body learned the cheers along with us, so that we could organize their shouting when the critical moment arrived, so that the effect would be multiplied again and again.

The pep rally had its own highs and lows, sobering moments when an injured hero was acknowledged, when the direness of the situation was explained by the coaches. Then the team was called out to the gymnasium floor in their sports coats and ties, where we led a cheer for them, attempting to fill up our team, contaminate them with pep, so that we could send them into battle brimming with encouragement.

During the chaos of the games, it was our job to transform the untrained and random sounds of the crowd—the frustrated voices shouting *C'mon* or *Air ball* or *Good job*—and harness them inside the amplified crucible of the gym into **De-**_fense,_ **De-**_fense,_ **stomp**-_stomp,_ **stomp**-_stomp-stomp,_ so that the words would break through and rearrange the heartbeats of our champions.

8.

The acoustic landscape of a basketball game is full of noise and cheers, wishes and curses. It's full of prayers, chants, and incantations, coming from all parties and moving in all directions. Fans scream and call and plead their way into the game. Athletes pray, and trash-talk, and wish, and curse—at each other, at the refs, into the ethers, into the heavens, calling on reserves, calling on favors.

Do these ur-utterances make a space where something happens? Before poems and prayers, there were spells and charms—carefully arranged words selected not only for their figurative and literal meanings, but also for their acoustic value, arranged and vocalized in specific, ritualized ways, so that they would travel as acoustic values through the waves of the world and effect change on the material plane.

9.

I'll admit I've imagined a world where poets would fill stadiums as athletes and rock stars now do. Where droves of people would fight traffic, take time off from work, to stand in line and rush to buy things that are far too expensive—tickets, T-shirts, beer, hot dogs—all the while wishing they could get back to their seats where they would scream and chant and cheer over a well-turned phrase, over the beauty of an image, the ingenuity of a metaphor.

I've imagined people so enraptured with poetry performances that they would recondition their RVs and show up early at stadiums, tailgating in cold parking lots, drinking beer and grilling burgers with total strangers, just so they could prolong the anticipation and the experience of hearing poetry read. Crazy talk, I know. But what is basketball but ten men in shorts, two empty baskets, and their desire to fill it with the one ball allowed in the game?

Imagine: *A poem is a closed and finite experiment designed to test the mettle and training, the natural talents and improvisational skills of its participants. The confines of the poem's structure create the effect of heightened drama, because, unlike life, every moment of a poem reminds us that something is at stake.*

10.

"Poetry makes nothing happen," Auden wrote. But what is the nothing about which Auden speaks? Does he simply mean that poetry doesn't fix potholes? That the world is made by the doers and that poetry has no effect or value in the material world?

Or when he speaks of the "nothing" that poetry makes happen, does he mean the expression of the rare and intangible thing, the ineffable, which is all around us but difficult to communicate because of its scale, especially with such small instruments as words and actions—like teaspoons measuring oceans. Most days, the magnitude registers as a void. Perhaps this is why prophets go to the desert, why tourists go to the Grand Canyon.

Sometimes, if the world goes silent for a moment we might cognize a small increment that intimates the largeness, but when we attempt to speak of it, the very sounding makes the ineffable move out of view. The words remain to remind us of the larger things that stand behind them in silence.

I've felt this absence of presence in rare moments after I've given a poetry reading or taught a class, when I prepare to leave the room, but look around one last time because I feel as if I've forgotten something there.

I've felt this presence, alone in the gym, after a long night of cheering, after things were decided and the game was won or lost—in the humming glare of the fluorescent lights, the gloss of the wax floor, the lingering smell of popcorn.

And I've observed it in the chaos of competition, in moments of near perfection that arrive with such elegance—the high diver's body entering the pool without a splash; the inaudible swish of the perfect jump shot.

Surely this is approaching the ineffable—to enter the water without the water knowing it, to put the ball through the hoop without troubling the net. It gives one hope. And surely this is what poets try for every day, arranging acoustic elegances that will intimate the magnitude. Surely this is what all the fuss—what all the cheering, the crying and gnashing of teeth—is all ultimately about.

THIRD QUARTER

FAST BREAK

WILLIAM HEYEN

I KNOW IT IN MY INTESTINES & IN MY BRAIN. I REALIZE IT WITH
what Emerson called "the flower of the mind."

We are coming to the end of all poetry.

Not just these word-constructs we read in books or once in a while hear
read aloud, but the way of thinking that integrates. The Concord master
said that the poet is the one who *integrates*, who intuits/knows/feels whole-
ness, interconnectedness.

By way of greed that seems often to dominate our nature, & by way
of various cause-&-effect specters—exploding population, deforestation/
desertification, extinctions, diminishing resources—we are coming to the
end of civilization & the tenure of the human species.

Maybe a fast nuclear or biological annihilation, maybe something somewhat slower. Kurt Vonnegut figured maybe a hundred years. Let's say five
hundred, but that's too soon enough, a blink in galactic time.

The end of poetry. The end of anthologies like the one you are holding in
hand. The end of playing fields & of arenas. The end of the nation-gathering

Olympic games & of all entertainments & sports. The end of basketball as we've known it.

But, first, this game that many of us love will come to accept more & more violence. The so-called civilized world becomes *Soylent Green, Escape from New York, Rollerball.* Do you remember heroes Thorne, Snake Plisskin, & who was the corporate athlete played by James Caan?

I've been an athlete all my life & still, at sixty-eight, play pickup basketball two or three times a week. (The young guys still like playing with me because I perform a maneuver they're not used to: the pass.) But over the decades I haven't written much about sports even though maybe I know more about the subject than I do about anything else. I played soccer, basketball, & baseball in high school; basketball & soccer (a two-time All American in soccer) in college; & I've played in many baseball & softball & basketball leagues since. As a professor, I taught Literature of Sport a few times. I've recently inhaled *DiMaggio: Setting the Record Straight* by Morris Engelberg & Marv Schneider, & Phil Jackson's *Sacred Hoops: Spiritual Lessons of a Hardwood Warrior,* and Mickey Mantle's own *The Mick*—some indication of some of the reading I keep doing. As a fan, I've rooted for the NFL Buffalo Bills here in western New York State—I'm one whose life has been involved with & enriched by sports. Now my four grandkids are on the fields & hardwood.

As I said, over the decades I haven't written much about this. But my poems "Mantle" & "The Stadium" have been in many anthologies, & many of the flash fictions in my one book of short stories, *The Hummingbird Corporation,* are sports-centered. A poem called "Parity" about a soccer game at Auschwitz is in *Shoah Train* & this basketball lyric appears in *The Confessions of Doc Williams & Other Poems*:

In the Country of Michelangelo

My friend Roosevelt Bouie—7-footer out of Syracuse,
passed up the NBA,

wanted to see the world, to meet all kinds of people,
so played pro ball in Italy,

once against Moses Malone. In a nasty exchange, Rosie's elbow
caught Moses flush on the temple,

knocked him cold. The man-mountain hit the floor, lay shuddering,
blood pooling under his head

from a wicked gash. When Rosie cared, he thought the flow
emanated from Moses's ear,

the sign, he'd heard, of a death-blow. Rosie himself almost passed out,
but medics got to work, stretcher-bearers

got Moses off the court, & he survived a concussion, a dozen stitches.
When Rosie told this story,

his voice became the prayerful whispers he'd heard from the stands,
but then the game resumed, Rosie

just going through the motions, wanting to stay out of the paint,
to avoid contact.

I've read this poem a hundred times now. I don't know what-all is going on in it. (A poem feels finished not just when its ideas have had their say but when there is rhythmical & aural closure.) But, after the instant of violence, prayer/conscience/reverence complicate the scenes. The poem asks to be read with "the flower of the mind" as my speaker remembers Rosie remembering something he'll never forget.

Often, we write about what we've lost or are losing. I can't see myself playing in the tough & serious basketball games I play in for more than a couple more years. But now I am slashing into shape a book of sixty to eighty poems on sport called *The Football Corporations* which takes place during apocalyptic times of dirty bombs going off at sports venues & of assorted other mega-catastrophes.

Now I remember: Caan plays Jonathan, our hero. I haven't seen the flick in years, but remember that last goal bashed into the throat of the corporation, & the crowd's shouted celebration of *Jon-a-than, Jon-a-than, Jon-a-than,* & the sleazy conspiratorial bigwigs going bananas as their program to rid the world of sanity & sportsmanship & individual freedom is at least momentarily thwarted by *Jon-a-than, Jon-a-than.*

In my book's last lyric, the Super Bowl, for the sake of political security, will be moved to the moon, but terrorists (vigilantes?) will strike there, too.

Remember Edward G. Robinson in *Soylent Green* (his last role, by the way, before he died of lung cancer)? He checks himself into a voluntary-death clinic, insists on the full (was it fifteen minutes?) time of TV nature scenery & symphony as the sedative & poison work in him.

What he sees—trees, a herd of deer, waves of birds—was once our world. Whitman prayed to nature for its "primal sanity."

And Cousy once played at Holy Cross & then for the Celtics. & verily came the time of Jordan/Magic/Bird/Jabbar, the age of controlled grace & power—I once saw Jerry West & Oscar Robertson team up as college all-Americans in an exhibition against the Knicks—that made us revere the game that we'll be losing to the violence & criminality that will increase upon itself to satisfy the corporation whose insensitized audience—I'm a *participant* in most of our worldly ills & excesses, but not in the desire for more mayhem in sports—wants more blood & breakage than finesse.

In her *Misogynies: Reflections on Myth and Malice,* reviewing many films, Joan Smith puts it simply: "a society inured to violent images of television requires bigger and bigger helpings of gore to raise a shiver." . . . Pro sports move toward Roman Coliseum spectacle.

Here's a new poem about a basketball superstar in our future. She'll appear in my forthcoming book of poems, *The Football Corporations.* She's got what it will take to get our attention, to evoke that shiver.

Chantel's Secret

Chantel, 6-11 franchise center, wheeled & slammed, then
elbowed her defender in the neck, but
didn't get ejected.

The Axis coach exploded, but the refs showed discretion,
didn't axe him—maybe they knew
they'd been too lax,

maybe intimidated by Chantel who spent
most of the second half taunting
the enemy bench

every time she backpedaled after scoring, which was often,
until after a last dunk when
a sub goon

undercut her. She went down like an imploding casino,
& caught fire, &, from her bra,
ex-

tracted a box-cutter, & went berserk—
she didn't kill anyone,
but cut tendons

& ligaments of two Axis benchwarmers
beyond repair despite even
the wonders

of modern sports bionics. She might miss half a season
during which ratings will decline,
but this time

the league's got to suck it up at least to *seem*
to be doing something.
Chantel

has not yet expressed regret—she's as stoic
an athlete as they come—
but this time

she'd best keep close to her entourage & guards
or the family of the maimed &/
or Axis fans

will take her out. All in all, it's a shame, isn't it,
that this fracas happened just before
the play-offs?—

now the record will need all sorts of asterisks.
We'd like to be mice under the table
at corporate quarters

when Chantel's endorsement contracts are renegotiated.
Little will change, though that negligee
might be a hard-on sell.

When you're writing a poem, you've got the ball & are driving toward the lane on a three-on-two fast break. You don't have any particular hard & fast plan in mind to execute, you're reacting rhythmically & opportunistically to what is around you & is trying to restrict you. Muscle memory after having been in this situation over the years. And sound memory: hear the catches at the back of the throat of this guy's language: neck, ejected, Axis, explored, coach, discretion, axe, lax, second, backpedaled, scoring, dunk, undercut, casino, caught, extracted, box-cutter, berserk, kill, cut, bionics, decline, suck, expressed, stoic, come, keep, close, take, fracas, record, asterisks, like, corporate, quarters, contracts. You're hearing everything as the story takes place by way of its sounds until, hopefully, one more sound, the *k*iss of the ball off the ba*ck*board.

I'm not sure who my speaker is, & he's not sure what is going on in corporation sports. & how can the tendon- & ligament-severing heroine be described as "stoic"? He's pretty much along for the ride. He cares more about the record book & the play-offs than about Chantel's victims. He doesn't say "hard sell" at the end—if he did, we'd still be within a milieu where morality & public disapprobation still held meaning—but "hard-on sell," & as I was driving to the end of this poem & the one word became the hyphenated adjective, I was in full subconscious awareness within Victoria's Secret advertising & the poetry game at the same time.

Writing this essay, executing a fast break, I realize that my fears about where we & basketball have been & where we & basketball are going—from country of the sacred to the corporation of the profane—is held within these two poems.

TIPPING OFF

LAUREN (JENTZ) JENSEN

AND WHAT TOOK PLACE OUTSIDE THE COURT WAS THAT AFTER WE
lost (yet another) close game to Reed City at home, the other starting post
player and I left through the back doors of Manistee High and drove down
to First Street Beach still in our jerseys, still with our ankles taped. We
couldn't quite shape words to whatever we were feeling, and ten years later,
I'm still not quite sure how to pin those emotions to the page.

Instead, what I have is a memory of that night: the way we kicked sand
on our way down to the shore of Lake Michigan, leaned our screen-printed
numbers against a piece of driftwood, and lit up the Virginia Slims we stole
from my mother's purse.

And that's what I remember. Not the score of the game, not even what
we talked about when we could finally talk, but just being there and the
sound of beach grass in the wind and the feeling of sand in the sweaty cracks
behind my knees. I'm addicted to the game itself, I LOVE basketball, but of
all the basketball I've played from 7th grade on through college, what keeps
the sport alive for me are seldom the things that surface in the news, have
found a place in the record books, or are even known. With that and as a

player, it makes me consider how much of the game, of poetry, seems to fall in the ruffled outskirts of the court or page.

I think about these unlit places often, and I'm thinking about them now, especially as I begin draft I'm-not-even-keeping-count-anymore of what you're reading and realize I've already written through so much (buzz of emergency lights in an empty gym vs. quiet before pen hits page) that will never make the cut. So while the ball may be figuratively tipped here, my attention still rests on less coordinated efforts, such as the warm-ups and practice and conditioning that it took for me to get to this moment.

Now, if this was an actual basketball game, here's the thirty-second time-out where I would be physically pulled from the court by my jersey and benched for looking for X cross court when I should have been watching for X cutting across the lane. However, this isn't an actual game (competition) and out of all the connections that naturally seem to exist between basketball and poetry (isn't everything eventually everything else anyway?) what I'm dueling with now is an actual place of disconnection. This being that on the court, we're always expected to perform, to play our best, play by the rules, and with poetry, with writing, I don't always find this the case, although these pressures are often felt and even more difficult to shake. And why is that?

Why is there a hesitation, a shimmy shake in sharing those oft sidelined failures and joys such as a luxury smoke after a tough loss? As I've said before and will say again, I love the actual game, I love competition, and I love the possibilities of playing on the big stage. But with writing, there's no running score, no final buzzer, and maybe (just maybe) there are no painted lines to isolate the action. In poetry, I have to remind myself of this: boundaries don't really exist and God Bless players like Apollinaire and Ashbery (along with many others whose names don't start with the letter "A" & of course Dr. J) who keep wide-eyed rookies like me from conforming to arbitrary rules and restrictions. Even then, preserve me in a way from feeling the pressure to be anything other than what I need to be with run-on sentences, awkward syntax, and asides. This is how I play.

And while I do believe (or am beginning to learn) there's a time and place to be polished and revised, I also fear too much of the practice, of the failures, of the laughter becomes lost in an emphasis to win, to please, and to be published. Sadly, it seems the later too often paints the lines by which some (young) poets play, instead of following intuition and remembering to find joy in what we do. And for me, it's the writing itself that remains most real—it's the attempt and often it's everything that falls outside and/or slips between the lines that ends-up feeling most alive. Even now, what you see here is the polished (as much as it could be) and what you don't see are all my initial digressions like when I used to sneak out the side door of our Victorian home on clear, crisp autumn nights.

[I would cross the street to Trinity Lutheran parking lot with my ball at hip until I reached the cracked blacktop and began the methodic back and forth, right and left dribble. As I moved closer to the hoop, I also moved closer to the church, and closer to the echo of the ball bouncing off the ground. Some nights I would just stand in one spot dribbling and listening to the counter noise, and other nights, I would reach the basket, let the ball roll off into dirt, and jump up to rattle the old chain-linked net. I spent unknown hours on this court with the wind in my pajamas, shooting free throws, and imagining big games that would come. They did come, but for some reason this is the place I return: the small beginning, where I still played even after my ball flattened on the colder nights and where I still aimed for the hoop even when blinded by car lights wrapping around Fourth Street onto Oak.]

Embedded in media, culture, and everyday conversation, people often make reference to the "world of sports" when in actuality this statement couldn't remain further from the truth. There is no *other* world separate from the oft referenced realm of sport; as there's no *other* world separate from poetry. There's just one world, and within that, the connected (collective) experiences are infinite and without restriction. However, what most fans and readers know of poetry and basketball is only what reaches center court, and this often excludes so much of what seems to really matter to us players, to me (the final day of try-outs where the *whole* team waited in the hall of the Dow Center knowing but ignoring the fact some of us wouldn't be handed a new pair of shoes, wouldn't play again).

It pains me that basketball and writing at times feel like diluted arts when what I want is the concentrated and fully realized. What I want is also something that may never be, but that's sports for ya, that's just all part of the dream and perhaps what keeps us coming back to the page: everything we can never attain. And for me, that everything feels the most possible just before the sit down, the tip-off, and I begin to write what's been in me for a long time or is around me now, immediate like the birds eating crumbs from my toast off a plate.

OFF THE RIM

ADRIAN MATEJKA

> *Layups. Fast breaks.*
> *We had moves we didn't know*
> *We had. Our bodies spun*
> *On swivels of bone & faith,*
> *Through a lyric slipknot*
> *Of joy, & we knew we were*
> *Both beautiful & dangerous.*

—"SLAM, DUNK, & HOOK," YUSEF KOMUNYAKAA

1. LAYUPS. FAST BREAKS.

When I was nineteen, the only thing that mattered as much as playing basketball was watching basketball. Indiana University in Bloomington, 1991, and the center of my campus was a monolith called the HPER. HPER is an acronym for School of Health, Physical Education, and Recreation, but for

123

me, it was the name of the first basketball facility where I could play ball as long and as often as I wanted for free.

The HPER was miraculous: rows and rows of basketball courts and at any time of any day, there were people playing. Most days, those people included me. Addressing Bertrand Russell's question, "Can human beings *know* anything?" in Philosophy class? Bertrand Russell was no Bill Russell, and discussing his hypotheses couldn't be as interesting as playing ball. Calculus quiz today? I'll be quizzing some scrub on how his ankles feel after I show him the chain rule of my crossover. Barely staying in school? That's okay, my three-point shot is like butter now and that's got to count for something.

English was the only subject I was able to manage reasonably because the professors left grading and attendance to the already overwhelmed graduate assistants. For most of those classes, all that was necessary for a decent grade was to turn in the essays. The exception was the class that should have been the easiest: Introduction to Creative Writing.

2. WE HAD MOVES WE DIDN'T KNOW / WE HAD.

Creative Writing was a class populated by the same students who turn up in every workshop:

1. A pale, nervous young woman who wrote diary entries about death and being side-swiped by love
2. A mumbler who never looked up from concocting phallic similes involving coffins and lipstick
3. An athlete (this time, a football player) looking to leap-frog Shakespeare for his English credits by writing haiku about the rigors of the field
4. Me, minority with a pen, fulfilling the quota

I was the personification of William Matthews's poem: "eighteen and miserable so I wrote a poem / and it was, of course, miserable." Even though the instructor said I was well-spoken, I didn't know anything about the craft of poetry. A line break may as well have been the necessary rest between line laps as far as I understood.

Even still, I was drawn to the idea of creativity. I didn't know anything about trying to create artistically, but I knew that creativity was an intangible that you either had or didn't have—like knowing when to cut for the bucket or when to fade to the top of the key. The thing that differentiated my poetic moves from the others in our class was that my writing was intuitively spiced with Black Arts rhetoric. After all, I was the token minority in class, just as I was the token nearly every place in Bloomington except the basketball court.*

It was my workshop leader who first suggested I speak with Yusef Komunyakaa. When I asked how to spell his last name, she said, "Don't worry about it. Everyone calls him 'Yusef.'" When I read a selection of his work in our class text, *New American Poets of the '90s,* the poems didn't much impress my raw sensibility. Other than "Venus's-flytraps," the narratives seemed like Adidas Top Tens, K-Tel hand-clap beats, or headbands: old school before old school was a good thing.

I later realized his poetry has a polyphonic swing, a lyrical motion through narrative that is so incredibly intricate that it at times seems easy—the same way a layup isn't all that impressive unless you take into account how many thousands of coordinated muscle movements are necessary for success.

3. SWIVELS OF BONE & FAITH, / THROUGH A LYRIC SLIPKNOT

I hadn't been to a professor's office yet, and I knew nothing of office hours or appointments, so I didn't know that it was inappropriate to demand an

---

* Comedians and bigots alike comment on the love of African-American men for basketball. While in Bloomington, I realized that playing basketball creates a community—even if that community only lasts until one of the teams wins the game—where there otherwise is none. This was especially the case in 1991, when there were barely enough African Americans at a university of almost forty thousand to run full court.

audience with a faculty member. I hadn't written more than ten pages of words—poetry or prose—either, so when I banged on that wooden door and the intense man opened it, I was not intimidated or impressed: a poet doesn't seem poetic until you know what poetry can be.

Yusef very politely told me to wait my turn and I agreed to do so. Not because his stature impressed, but because he had mentioned the Lone Ranger—my favorite black-and-white television character when I was a child—in one of his poems. And there was something rumbling in his words—and his accent, which was the verbal equivalent of a seventies strut, all smoothed and tilted—that made me think that talking with him might be a good thing.

It's exactly right that Yusef was working on the concept for *Talking Dirty to the Gods* while in Bloomington. The book both glorifies and questions the underbelly of mythology (poetic or otherwise) and there was a mythos surrounding him at Indiana University, even before he won the Pulitzer.

His appearances never caused anyone to cancel class like one of Bob Knight's open practices, but his free readings at the Runcible Spoon became social events more like concerts than poetry readings. The readings were meant to help the coffee shop stay in business by bringing in the coffee-buyers and getting there early was a must: a few hours in advance for a seat, at least an hour early for a spot inside. Latecomers were relegated to the outside, where speakers that sounded like someone holding up a phone to a jukebox amped whatever was going on in the back room. But they'd stay out there, listening, whether the snow was shoveled or not.

Appreciating none of this at the time, I returned to his office after a cup of coffee at the Runcible Spoon, having reread my fistful of poems. The first thing I said to him was, "Yusef, when you read my poems and see how good they are, will you kick one of the students out of your writing class so I can be in?"

I was so intent on delivering my loud-mouth declaration that I didn't even notice that his office hours were already over; that he was in the middle of writing a poem when I banged on the door; that I didn't really believe my poems were that good; and that creative writing workshops at Indiana are not merit-based. Unlike pickup ball, the classes are filled on a first-come, first-served basis, with little consideration to skill. I couldn't see any of this because I approached writing and talking about poetry in the same way I approached basketball: in order to get picked up for a game, you have to act like you can play.

It was only in retrospect that the validity of Yusef looking at me at first as if I owed him money became clear. Then he smiled and said simply, "You know . . . everyone thinks they're good" and asked if I had poems to show him. "No, not with me," I said as I backed toward the door thinking, *This old man just punked me out* . . .

4. & WE KNEW WE WERE / BOTH BEAUTIFUL & DANGEROUS.

I spent the next three years working on my poetic chops. I was going to show Yusef who was good. I cut my basketball playing down to roughly four days a week. I rarely went out with my friends. I spent hours listening to The Pharcyde, Fela Kuti, and Miles Davis, trying to find a way to distill their music into words. I read and reread *Magic City* looking for the right words to distill. I'd show Professor Yusef Komunyakaa the difference between somebody with game and somebody who thinks he has game.

During that time, I learned a bit more about poetry and about the uniqueness of Yusef's poetic statements. I learned how a poem's logic can tattoo itself into the brain so that "She burns" must be followed with "like a burning bush / driven by a godawful wind." Or why it just makes sense that "August is a good time / for a man to go crazy," especially in the Midwestern humidity.

But no amount of reading or admiration for the power of his poetry could slow my urge for a rematch with Yusef. Even if I did hide behind the first available tree every time I saw him walking across campus, scribbling in his notebook. Even if I couldn't write a poem about basketball because "Slam, Dunk, & Hook" said all I had to say about hoops.

In the fall of my second senior year, I was ready: with sheaf of poems in my clutch, I registered for Yusef's workshop. He'd just won the Pulitzer for *Neon Vernacular.* When I walked into his class, ready to represent, he wasn't even there. Roger Mitchell, the head of the MFA program, was the last-minute replacement because Yusef was on sabbatical. He didn't return until after I'd graduated.

In 2002, I had the good fortune to finally study with Yusef at Cave Canem, a writer's retreat for African American poets. It was the first time I had spoken with him since I ran out of his office eleven years before. He had just judged the Bakeless Prize, for which my manuscript was a finalist but didn't win. So I still felt the need to show him that I had poetic skill.

Even before I'd turned in my hoop gear for (what I thought was) good during graduate school, I had come to realize how impressive a writer Yusef is. His poetic rockings between demons and drums make their own unique lyric and narrative concoction—one whose complexity has both confused and invigorated me more than that of any other poet. What I mistook as being an old-school aesthetic at nineteen was, in fact, Yusef breaking aesthetic's ankles.

When I caught up with Yusef on the first day of the Cave Canem, after having several years of reflection on how I'd unintentionally disrespected him, there was a whole lot more hat in my hand than there had been at our first meeting. He somehow remembered our brief encounter, though not as graphically as I did ("Did I say that?" he asked with a smile), but his response to my questions about my manuscript was more detailed.

We talked for about two hours, and he spent that time pointing out some of the fundamental things in the manuscript that weren't effective—from the opening poem to the arrangement of the sections. We talked about approach and intent, writing rhetoric and the basics of poetry. One of the most important suggestions he gave me was about the working title, "The Nature of Skin." Yusef told me straight up, "Change it. There are too many books of poetry around with 'skin' in the title." Later that week, he compounded things by pointing out that "a bad title is like a dunce cap on a poem."

I'd spent a very long time trying to come up with a poetic title for my book, and an equally long time trying to come up with a poetic sensibility for myself. But Yusef's dunce cap simile reminded me of an experience at a basketball camp I attended as a teenager. Steve Alford—the hardworking jump shooter who would lead Indiana University to a NCAA title in 1987—preached to us the importance of persistence, of addressing the fundamentals.

He said, "Practice free throws and jump shots every day. You never know when you'll get the chance to shoot a layup, but you can always shoot a jump shot." I wasn't even beginning to hear what Alford was saying; in my mind, jump shots were for people who didn't have enough game to shoot any other way. But what was impressive about Alford's talk was that he wasn't a disembodied lecture, detached from his subject matter. The whole time he was speaking, he was also shooting free throws—one hundred straight without a miss, "Nothing but a hot / Swish of strings like silk."

Like Alford, Yusef is teacher, practitioner, and walking example of tenacity. Asked once what he wanted his work to be remembered for, he said, "Persistence." Indeed, Yusef's success can be attributed in part to his relentless follow-through: his refusal to turn away from any of the possibilities in poetic invention, whether manifested as freewheeling verbs, imagistic improvisation, or trocheed aggression. That poetic persistence can create possibility is something Yusef unconsciously introduced me to in Bloomington and reiterated at Cave Canem. It may be true that everyone thinks they are good, but Yusef Komunyakaa's poetry—his willingness to share and instruct—proves time and time again that he is the one who truly has game.

COURTING RISK

Thoughts on Basketball and Poetry

PATRICIA CLARK

IT'S DARK AND PROBABLY RAINY, THE KIND OF SOFT DRIZZLY RAIN
Seattle did not invent but shares with Ireland, with London and Amsterdam. I have been walking north on Fifteenth Avenue Northeast from my
dorm because it's still dark out and this route is well lit. Now, almost to NE
Forty-fifth Street, I make a right turn, climb a short flight of cement stairs
from sidewalk to tree-lined parking lot, and am finally on the University
of Washington campus. I am hurrying to be on time for a 7:00 A.M. class,
Introduction to Basketball.

I cut across a large parking lot near the Burke Museum, lift my hand in a
wave to the guard in the traffic hut at the campus entrance and go scurrying
on past rhododendrons that tower over me, though this morning I do not
notice their color. I smell leaf mold, damp blossoms, and evergreen before
I give a quick yank to the door of Hutchinson Hall, bustling down the corridor with a couple other just-arrived students. Today we start in a regular

classroom—on alternate days, as I am about to discover, we will meet in the locker room and suit up.

Basketball and poetry. The first one I know little about, and the other I have spent thirty-some years studying and writing. With poetry I have worked in the fields, so to speak, as a practitioner in the garden of poetry—sowing seeds, tilling and weeding, occasionally reaping the fruits, biting into a delicious finished poem, reveling in the experience of something new (either my own or someone else's), experiencing the juice, the pleasure, of a "finished" object, a book of poems, say, that especially tender ripe fruit. I see the tawny yellow-peach blush of an apricot. With basketball I have been largely an onlooker—yet people come to mind, some sharply, some more shadowy, and a sense of pleasure and tension—excitement, a thrill. Figures swirl into mind—tall figures in basketball gear. Someone drives for a layup, and there is ballet in the length of the strides, the leap, the flinging of the ball. Another player who has made it look easy: deceptive in the physical game on the court. Have I reached the point where writing would appear to come easily for me?

I have never been a player of team sports. Even badminton, a game I came to love and played when I was at Stadium High School in Tacoma, Washington, had been singles, not doubles. As a teenager, I kept on the move physically though it was not an era when girls were especially encouraged to do sports, especially team sports. I see myself in two seasons: summers at Sandy Beach in a bikini and long T-shirt cover-up doing the strange activity we called "piko boarding." This involved throwing a thin wooden or plastic disk large as a trash can cover down on the filmy saltwater, an eighth of an inch left when the tide went out at the beach. One flung the disk down, then ran and jumped on, skidding and flying ahead across the sand. Alternatively, in winter, I fancied myself a downhill skier, rode the group bus to Crystal Mountain resort with friends, subscribed to *Ski* magazine, all while fantasizing that a broken leg would be an attractive lure for boys. Helpless damsel in distress, I would let a favorite pen his name on my cast in these fantasies. On the ski bus I fell under the influence of Marcia Pearson—a fast blonde at Stadium High School. She had a flask and we made whiskey snow cones to get up our courage for particularly steep or icy runs.

In the late 1960s at the University of Washington, physical education was a yearlong requirement (the year divvied up in quarters, the system U of W used then). In fact, it was also a co-requirement in this land of saltwater beaches, bays, and inlets of Puget Sound, plus many freshwater lakes, that all students demonstrate the ability to swim. If you couldn't prove it, you took a class. I could already swim so I signed up for basketball. Sailing also intrigued me but the time commitment was bigger and I had an afternoon job. Was there some other reason I signed up for basketball? And did I really think I would make it to a 7:00 A.M. class?

In the shadows of memory, I can barely make out the classroom—just an older brick building with nondescript pale yellowing walls and desks in rows. A teacher who I can no longer see or hear. A handout: a surprisingly detailed syllabus, the course requirements, attendance policies, dates of written midterm and final exams, and then the equipment requirements. Navy shorts, plain white tee, and shoes worn only here. I was a poor work-study student toiling twenty hours a week in the Department of Urology, always strapped for cash. I almost considered dropping the class but I had a charge account at the University Bookstore and they sold a lot of gear so I knew I could get the clothes. For good or ill, I stayed in the class.

I wonder what my sense was, at eighteen years old, of what I wanted to do with my life? I fear that looking back, that 20/20 hindsight, all looks very neat and orderly, even rational. In many ways, I felt defined by what I did not want to be: like my mother. Dinner is over at our house in Browns Point, and my mother is in the kitchen, making coffee and cleaning up. My father, brothers, brothers-in-law—they are all in the living room, talking politics. I wanted to live a different kind of life than being a wife and mother—I wanted to be in the living room talking about politics rather than washing off plates and putting them in the dishwasher. It was the era of feminism and I hated the word "girl"—even had a big fight with a brother-in-law of mine who used the word carelessly.

I was ready to take a risk. The same brother-in-law I quarreled with had been a major encouragement to me: "Go to college," he urged me on more than one occasion. And: "That Bob you're dating. You can do better." Anyone who chooses to be a writer, an artist of any kind, must possess a level of tolerance for risk—as well as a tolerance for rejection. What else might be in the future for a writer? Some poverty, no doubt, as well as uncertain employment. Similar, I would suppose, with those who go for a life in professional sports. Play ball as a career choice? Write poetry? Did a relative really say to me, "What are you going to do—hang out a shingle? Poems written here?" I was lucky not to have parents who would say, "Are you kidding?" After all, I was a girl. A career or education did not really matter for a girl because it was considered she would marry and be taken care of. How contradictory: it was insulting, but in another sense, this role granted immense freedom.

Here's the voice of our teacher-coach coming in loud: "Line up for drills: two rows, you here, you there. Dribble the ball, move down the court, take a shot, pass off to the next girl, and back." Whirls of color in action, squeak of shoes, the orange hard ball. I could use some practice on the dribble, that's for sure. "C'mon, girls! Hup, move it, let's move!" Turns out, it's important to know how to dribble the ball without looking at it. Who knew? I was lucky to be able to dribble, awkwardly, with eyes fastened on the ball. Clearly some of these girls had played before; but I had not. It must be our first day on the court. My gym years in the past had not been stellar ones—memories of Gray Junior High and many admonitions and correction for anything I did: rope climb or volleyball, sit-ups or posture. I was a bookworm; this was not my place. Cotton bibs to tie over your T-shirt—some red, some blue. Teams: *Sue, you be the red captain; Jo, you're the blue. Now choose your squad. The rest of you can warm the bench and rotate in.*

General education is part of most undergraduate liberal arts curriculum; or, Gen Ed, as everyone calls it. As a professor now I speak heartily in favor of it to reluctant students: "As a citizen, a voter, you need a bit of science. You'll have to vote on environmental issues and the like." And physical education? I would speak in favor of it, too, though these requirements have long since been dropped. As a writer I have found over and over again the sweet tandem activities of writing with something more physical. A morning at the desk, an afternoon of gardening.

I write in a small studio at the edge of our property, at the tipping point down to a ravine and Lamberton Creek behind our house. A space heater chugs along keeping me warm in winter and a ceiling fan spins lazily overhead in warmer times. Two of the windows open. In the mornings, I start at seven-thirty or eight, working steadily till noon if I can. Then, in gardening season, it's time to put in a flat of impatiens near the front walk, or situate some new hostas I found for our shady backyard. My friend Dale knows all the hosta names: Sum & Substance, Blue Mouse Ears, Dorset Blue, Twilight. In that long ago time at the University of Washington I barely had time for anything after classes, studying, a job. I was not interested in gardening yet—it reminded me too much, still, of my mother—who had a green thumb. By the end of my freshman year at the University of Washington, by May of 1970, no physical education requirement remained. Intro to Basketball was the last PE class I ever took.

Maybe my interest in basketball had something to do with the Boston Celtics and Bill Russell. My mother was a Bostonian, long-removed from Massachusetts to live in the Pacific Northwest—but her Boston accent and our Irish uncles, aunts, and cousins allowed us to claim Boston as a second home. We rooted for Boston teams with the best of them: the Red Sox and, of course, the Celtics. Bill Russell (#6) was the dominating player at center there in the mid to late 1960s. When Wilt Chamberlain was drafted and joined the Philadelphia Warriors in the 1959–1960 season, there was a decade-long rivalry between Chamberlain and Russell. Then, in 1966–67 Russell became the first player-coach in NBA history. There was something about Bill Russell that charmed that high school girl in Tacoma: he had a devilish twinkle in his eye and an articulateness that sparkled as well. Go to YouTube now and look at 2009 interviews with Bill Russell and tell me you are not wowed by what you see and hear. It isn't simply charisma, either; it is ethics, integrity, humor. Maybe, too, I was intrigued in some of those tumultuous years by Russell's disillusionment with the Vietnam War and his sorrow over the assassinations of Martin Luther King, Jr. and Robert Kennedy. Apparently the Eastern Division Finals in the NBA were going on that spring, when on April 4, 1968, Martin Luther King, Jr., was assassinated. Calls to cancel the games went unheeded. Russell and his teammates were depressed and playing lackluster ball because of it. The Celtics ended up in a 3–1 deficit against the Philadelphia Sixers with no one believing they could battle back from such a deficit. Somehow they did, and Bill Russell went on to be named *Sports Illustrated*'s "Sportsman of the Year."

By my second year at University of Washington I had gained more credits and also found a boyfriend—and a very athletic one at that. J. S., as I'll call him here, radiated physical prowess. For one thing, he was commandingly tall: six feet, five inches at least. He had massive thighs, seemingly as big around as my waist, and shopped for his clothes at the Big & Tall shop in Seattle. J. S. played basketball and wanted, passionately, to be a professional basketball player. He had started college on the other side of the state, by the waving, golden wheat fields of the Palouse, at Washington State University, before transferring to the University of Washington. He had tangled at WSU with Coach Jud Heathcote when J. S. played on what I seem to remember was the junior varsity team. At some point, Heathcote had told him flat out that he was not good enough to make the varsity team at WSU, and not tall enough, if that was his dream, for the NBA. Bad things happened at WSU with Jud Heathcote and my friend, though so many years later I do not remember what it was. I think it had something to do with being aggressive on the court. My boyfriend abhorred violence and was more likely to walk away from a confrontation than elbow into one. I think he sat on the bench once too often at WSU, burning and fuming. Before long, he had left and come to the U of W. The refrain in his head even then, "You're not tall enough for the NBA."

Here a quick figure with a shiny bald head and white headband whirls and dribbles into view, moving sideways and up, around other players, before they can stop him. It's 1973 and the team is the Seattle SuperSonics. It's no longer my sophomore year, and J. S. and I are still together, watching basketball when we can. He plays at the University of Washington's Intramural Activities Building, known as the IMA, on Montlake Boulevard. Pickup games, and formal intramural teams. I remember going to pick him up there one day when he sprained his ankle. Together we come to love this Sonics player, or maybe I am the one intrigued enough by this player to remember his name and profile so many years later. He is Donald Earl Watts, known by fans and admirers as "Slick" Watts. In contradictory personal stats, whether you believe the NBA site or Wikipedia, he is either six foot, one inch, or a flat, steady (and short) six foot even. As number 13 for the Sonics, in 1976 Slick Watts would lead the NBA in a whopping four categories: total assists, assists per game, total steals, steals per game, plus that year he made the NBA All-Defense First Team. "But he's a point guard," J. S. kept saying to me. "Don't you get the difference? I don't have any training as a guard. I play center." As it turns out, Slick ended up with quite a short NBA career—he only played six NBA seasons before retiring. The last I heard, due to a flattering reminiscence of him in the *Seattle Times*, Watts was teaching PE at Brighton Elementary in Seattle's Rainier Valley.

Long after knowing someone, it's interesting how much one recalls about the defining moments of another person's life. They seem far clearer than the defining moments of one's own. Basketball, and his inability to go farther with it, had been the second bitter pill in J. S.'s life—one never to be gotten over, after his parents' divorce—basically, his mother's betrayal of his father through an extramarital affair. Not tall enough? He told me that 6'5" was good enough only if you were a guard, and only if you were a guard of the talent and quickness of Slick Watts or Jerry West. J. S. went on to major in history and was brilliant, I thought, at European intellectual history. But ultimately he chose to pursue a career in library science instead of history. He had seen his stepfather finish a PhD in Latin American history and not be able to find full-time employment. J. S., by contrast, would go for a sure thing.

I watch Bill Russell hamming it up with four sports commentators on YouTube. His infectious laugh is still there, causing them all to giggle and crack up. After all his awards and honors, what is Russell most proud of? "I am my father's son," he says soberly. "My father told me he was proud of me, and that made all the difference in the world." Coming out of college, playing basketball, he relates how he had three offers: to play ball in Europe, to join the Harlem Globetrotters, or to play in the NBA. The NBA offer was the lowest one, financially, but it's the one he chose: "I was all about competition," Russell says with a grin. Speaking of another championship game, he tells of the players lined up on the other side against him and his team. Ultimately, though, he claims, "We beat them like they were ugly stepchildren." That laugh again, the whole set erupting in laughter.

How to set a pick. These words from my Intro to Basketball class so many years ago have stayed with me. Beyond the context, the words mean little to me. From Internet research I know that setting a pick is a key tactic in basketball. As a teacher, I see the phrase now as a cautionary "note to self": your students might remember you and forget the lesson. Those of us, though, who recall fabulous teachers (and perhaps hope to be remembered in some nearby category or other) will hear their voices coming through loud and strong. One brief anecdote about poet Richard Hugo, with whom I studied at the University of Montana, earning an MFA before going on to Houston. Hugo had advised me against pursuing a PhD. I think the quote was, "They'll ruin your writing." I was stubborn, though, and determined; plus I had my reasons. "Okay, then, if you're going to go, I think the University of Houston is the place for you. Stanley Plumly is there, and I think he can teach you a thing or two," Hugo said in his office one day. He made Houston sound like the land of milk and honey: "There's money there for graduate students." With his blessing, I was off.

Phi Slama Jamma. This was the University of Houston's fraternity of players who went on to two rounds of Final Four play in the NCAAs, in 1983 and 1984. Who knew I would end up, in the next phase of my life, in Houston, Texas, studying creative writing? The joke I made for years, coming to Texas from all my previous twenty-eight years in the Pacific Northwest, was that I had never been entirely warm in my whole life. Houston and its muggy atmosphere took care of that. As for college basketball, I had been watching the NCAA games for years with J. S. In fact, I think we even watched NIT (National Invitation Tournament) games. But now I had a ringside seat to watch the best team in the country—or just about. In fact, Akeem Olujawon and Clyde ("The Glide") Drexler could also be seen strolling the campus past the regular mortals who were the rest of us. Some of my colleagues at U of H even taught Cougar basketball players in Basic English classes. I recall hearing tales of how Olujawon and others folded their tall figures into the small ordinary side desks in Cullen Hall. The green areas near that building, with stately gnarled oaks hung with Spanish moss, come back to me and a vision of the '65 Plymouth Valiant I still drove there. It had been J. S.'s stepfather's car. Now I saw up close, certainly closer than ever before, some seasons of near victory and close defeat: The Cougars would lose to North Carolina State's Wolfpack and Lorenzo Thomas in 1983 and to Georgetown's Patrick Ewing in 1984. It was years before I could grudgingly admire Ewing's fabulous athletic abilities.

Now it's post-Houston, and I've moved to Knoxville, Tennessee. I am surrounded by wonderful colleagues at UT-Knoxville and have grown especially fond of some of my fellow short-term friends in the English Department: adjuncts, instructors, visitors, and the like. Someone organizes an office pool to bet on the NCAA games. It's February: spring, renewal, my birthday, and I'm taking flying lessons in single-engine planes at a nearby airfield. Someone prods me, one afternoon, to enter the pool. I sit down five minutes before the deadline and choose teams in various brackets. Once I have my choices, I have the good sense to Xerox my ballot—I'm going to need to remember these picks as I watch the tournament. I settle in, nightly, to watch the NCAA games. Over and over, I have chosen correctly. Each time there is an upset, somehow I have chosen the winning team. I take it as a sign, all the while wishing my poetry life would go as easily.

It's 1989 and I have just been offered a tenure-track job: I will be moving to Grand Rapids, Michigan, in the summer to start as an assistant professor at Grand Valley State University. In the intervening years, I have finished my PhD at Houston and written a creative dissertation of poems, complete with critical introduction where I place my work on the timeline of American literature. Continuing to publish poems in magazines, I am frustrated at times with the difficulty of finding a publisher for a book of poems. Over the years my poetry manuscript comes in as a finalist at so many places that I am tantalized and annoyed. What I had thought would be so simple—the risks I was taking to choose to be a poet—now seems infinitely harder and more complicated than I imagined. Publishing is one thing, and what about writing? That seems harder, too. I am teaching four classes a term at UT-Knoxville; not simple to keep the creative juices flowing with all that instruction, all that paper grading. And even with some time squeezed out to write: who are the poetic role models, now, after graduate school? Remembering Dick Hugo, I think, "Can I get the taste of graduate school out of my mouth?" It was mostly positive, a wonderful fellowship found, at times, among graduate students. The comments in workshops were extremely critical—not on a personal level—and the level of critique stayed with me: the standard is high for good writing. Sometimes, though, among the teachers and their followers—well, let's just say there was competition and some talk of "Who's the number one student?"

Certainly risk-taking is an essential trait in choosing to be a writer, and in continuing to write and to confront the blank page. What liberates us to take such risks, or what holds us back? I am not looking back to fault my friend J. S. for not pursuing his dream; for whatever reasons, it was not possible for him. No doubt my ability to take a risk in choosing writing was aided by social times (the late 1970s, early 1980s) and also by my coming from a large family. I was not expected to succeed with a profession, and there was ironic freedom there. Who knows what else is in the mix, from genetic makeup to ability to tolerate uncertainty and discomfort. How does one learn to launch into the unknown as a writer? To take leaps—as though one were a dancer. The physical risks of playing professional ball seem huge, and I think, too, of the psychological aspects of the game, intimidation, psyching out one's opposition—though I am admittedly not an insider to this element of the game. What is the equivalent with writing, I wonder? Not a team sport, that's for sure. One spends time confronting the white space of the page (or the computer monitor) and, perhaps, voices in one's head. Is one in competition with fellow writers? I have often heard the advice, "Don't read your contemporaries but read the masters." Is this what it's all about—psyching oneself out? Then there is the job world of writing and of sports. It seems the tenure-track job race has gotten more and more competitive because of recent economic bad times. Competition for a job cannot be any easier in the NBA.

Aren't there, realistically, many ways of loving an art, a game: intimately and deeply, or from the sidelines? And not an either/or, one or the other, but many gradations in between. Many levels of seriousness on which to play or make one's mark. Often, surely, it is people that draw us to such passionate intensity: hearing a poet read, as I heard Philip Levine in Port Townsend, Washington, at the Centrum Foundation Conference in 1976, breaking up the audience with his comments between poems. It was a bombshell moment for me. Here's what I remember thinking: "If a man can choose to write poetry and take it this seriously, wow! Then this is indeed a serious business." Maybe if my friend J. S. had encountered Slick Watts at a basketball camp, his life path might have been different.

In that 1989 office pool I made some lucky choices. Most particularly, bravely, foolishly, because I was moving to Michigan, I picked the University of Michigan to win it all. Serendipity, a lark, beginner's luck, foolish ignorance. I put all my money on them to win. And they did. As for that 7:00 A.M. Intro to Basketball class—I attended all quarter, missed a few classes and probably stayed up all night more than once to make sure I made it to Hutchinson Hall. Our teacher gave us a fifteen-page final exam. To this day, it is *how to set a pick* that has stayed with me; that and how difficult it is to dribble a ball without looking. After some thirty-plus years writing sentences and hoping to craft them into poems, I am still looking at the ball sometimes; other times, like maybe one morning this week—I write some lines and have the effortless feeling of floating, words coming out of my pen unbidden, unforced. In fact, I'm not even sure the hand at work is my own.

BASKETBALL, FAILURE, AND
AMATEUR PLEASURE

JEFF GUNDY

WHAT IS IT ABOUT BASKETBALL? SOMEONE ONCE POINTED OUT THAT it's ridiculous to have a sport in which games are regularly decided by something like one one/hundredth of the total points scored. After a 106–105 game, how can we really say that one team is better than the other? Maybe that capacity for razor-thin margins is part of its appeal. So many things happen over the course of a truly competitive game, so many small successes and failures, so many points scored and shots made and missed; of all the major sports, it seems somehow the thickest with events, the most dependent on the accumulation of minor results rather than on one or two spectacular plays. Bad basketball games can be astoundingly, transcendentally dull, but the best ones generate a particular kind of drama that nothing else can quite match.

Almost anybody can play basketball; unlike football, it takes very little equipment besides a court, and unlike baseball, it provides vigorous aerobic exercise. (John Kruk is once supposed to have remarked, "I'm not an athlete, lady. I'm a baseball player.") Tall people have an obvious advantage, but anyone who is reasonably coordinated and not too slow can learn to dribble and shoot and pass and play some sort of defense. But like anything else, being really *good* is another story. And because basketball teams are small, the number good enough to keep playing organized basketball is also small, and the number of frustrated former basketball players, those whose active playing days ended before they were really ready, is especially large.

I suppose it goes almost without saying that I am one. I started playing outside in the yard and on the playgrounds and gyms of my little town as soon as I could heave the ball up to the rim (none of those adjustable models in my day—it was the whole ten feet or forget it). We had several hoops out on the farm, at various times—first on the old garage, where there was pretty good gravel to the right but only grass on the left, which made dribbling difficult. Later my dad moved it to the side of the barn, where there was a concrete slab that was almost smooth. My brother Gregg and I played one-on-one out there all through one Christmas vacation when there was no snow on the ground, learning to hoist jump shots against the resistance of hooded sweatshirts. He was five years younger, but I could already tell he was going to be better at it than me.

The dark though not unusual secret of my basketball career is that I was never very good at it. Too short to guard most others, relatively quick but not deft or sure enough with the ball to play point guard—where was I going to play?

That didn't keep me from trying, naturally. And my home town was small enough that kids like me got some kind of chance. I played all through grade school, and the peak of my career came in the eighth grade. Back in the sixties Illinois had a very strange class system for grade-school basketball. Each school could have two teams, but rather than dividing them by grades or ability, an arcane formula involving height, weight, and birth date decided who was a "Lightweight" and who a "Heavyweight." In eighth grade I was just short enough and young enough to play on the Lightweights, which meant that for the last time in my life none of the other players were much taller than me.

I was a starter that year, for the first and last time in my life, and we had a pretty good team—if I remember right, we went 11–4. I averaged seven or eight points, third on the team, not so bad for twenty-four-minute games, and got a little trophy for having the best free throw percentage, somewhere around 65.

My very best moment came in the district tournament at the end of the season. We won our first game, maybe even two, but in the championship we fell ten points behind a team from a much bigger school. In the fourth quarter we put on a desperate press and began a nothing-to-lose comeback. We got into the zone, and the other team started to get a little rattled—as everybody who plays basketball knows, momentum is everything, and sometimes it's easier to play from behind than to protect a lead.

Slapping at every ball and trying to intercept every pass, running at every chance and hitting some unlikely shots, we came almost all the way back. All at once, with just a few seconds left, we were just two points behind. I was not generally our first option, but somehow I got the ball on the right side, put it on the floor and got right to the rim. I ball-faked and somebody jumped all over me; no chance to get the shot off, but the whistle blew. Timeout. Four seconds on the clock.

The coach—a balding, gruff but not mean guy who understood us well—spent the whole timeout talking about setting up the defense after the free throws. Only as we were heading back onto the court did he say something brief and matter-of-fact to me—"Put 'em in," maybe.

Somehow it didn't even occur to me to be nervous. I went through my routine—placed my feet, took the ball, took three dribbles, bent my knees—and put the first one right over the front of the rim. I suppose people cheered, but I didn't notice, and this was before players slapped hands between every free throw, made or missed. I just waited for the ball to come back, went through my routine again, and put the second shot in exactly the same spot, just over the rim and through the net. This time I did notice people yelling, in a vague way, and I thought something like "How about that?" as I slid back to play defense for the last seconds.

The other team didn't get a shot off before the buzzer. We crushed them in overtime, and celebrated like mad. Afterwards, my mother confessed that she didn't really expect me to make the free throws, which surprised me—it had never even occurred to me that I might miss one.

Next came the regional; I remember sitting through the long drive in the rear-facing backseat of the coach's station wagon with a couple of my pals, still feeling special. We got clobbered, made the long drive again for the third-place game, and got clobbered again. It hardly mattered.

But then it was high school, and no more lightweights. I played some on the freshman team—I remember scoring the first basket of one game on a baseline jumper—but the growth spurt I was hoping for never came. I hurt my knee at the end of football my sophomore year and missed the first part of basketball; I came back with my knee heavily taped and often painful, and mostly rode the junior varsity bench. I had plenty of time to think about how to play the game, but it didn't help me any out on the floor. When the season ended, the coach suggested, not unkindly but crushingly, that I probably ought to figure out some other way to keep myself occupied next winter.

So I joined the legions of former basketball players earlier than many; no inspirational Michael Jordan stories for me. I didn't stop loving the game, but I switched mostly to spectating, which has its own rewards and requires no particular skills. I got really good at the dubious art of yelling at referees during our high school games, where I cheered on my classmates and former rivals for playing time. My senior year, at the coach's request, I started recording play-by-play of the varsity games—in the era before video—though I was never sure how often the coach actually listened to them, or what good they did him. I sat with the stat crew in a little corner on the visitor end of the gym, which mainly worked out fine. One of my Lightweight teammates was on the crew—like me, retired young from organized basketball. He also sometimes played the national anthem on his trumpet. After one win against a big rival, he pulled the trumpet out again and played "Taps" while the crowd was still shuffling out, which got us some threatening gestures . . . but no fight. We were pretty moderate boys in those days, really.

After high school I played pickup ball once in a while. When I got my first teaching job in Kansas I joined a group that played noon-hour basketball two or three times a week, partly for the exercise, partly because I still loved the game. There were some good players—two guys who had played for one of the state schools in Kansas, along with their dad, who was fifty-ish but still rock-solid, and a lot of former high school players. I was still marginal, but usually there was somebody at about my level when it came time to divide the teams, and nobody got too worried about my tendency to brick shots and my lack of a vertical leap. After running around for an hour I was so full of endorphins that I didn't even mind being sweaty and hungry all through my one-o'clock class.

I also played some on the faculty intramural team. One night we played a student team that included one of my advisees who had been cut by the basketball coach, who was our best player. Joe was on a mission that night—he must have scored thirty points, though he didn't say a word to the coach, and we lost by about that much.

When I moved to Ohio, the noon-hour basketball ended; the pickup games at the local rec center were at six in the morning, way too early for me. I played intramural for a few years, but it was too late at night and too sporadic, and eventually I turned to jogging and handball for more regular exercise. My boys grew up playing soccer, mostly, their tentative basketball forays not much more successful than my own. Now, in my midfifties, my main handball partner moved away, I've more or less given up competitive sports in favor of straight-line activities that keep my knees mostly pain-free.

Still, I talk about basketball in class a good deal. When I am trying to convince my writing students that practice is more important than "creativity," sports and music are my two main resources for metaphors and analogies. Did Michael Jordan or Larry Bird invent the jump shot? I ask them. Grammar is like dribbling, I tell them: nobody will notice much if you've mastered it, but if you haven't, you'll look like a fool.

Then there's the great American myth that we all can be "whatever we want to be." When I ask a first-year class about this, most of them generally agree that it's so. My follow-up question is always "So how come I'm not in the NBA?" A good discussion about the limits and restraints on sheer wish and desire generally ensues, as long as I don't overreact to the "vertically challenged" remarks.

What does basketball have to do with poetry? Both are endeavors that a whole lot of people can do in an amateur way. How many Americans have made at least one basket, and written at least one piece of writing that might be labeled a poem? Both are extremely hard to do well enough to get paid—but then, that's true of most human endeavors. Those who succeed at both tend to have a great deal of innate ability and the drive to work extremely hard.

But maybe the most intriguing similarities are not at the extremes, but in the middle ranges. You don't have to play basketball well to take great pleasure in it—and it is good for you, too. The physical benefits diminish when you can't take the floor any more, but you don't even have to play to love the game. Even the inevitable failures and losses, the repeated reminders of how radically the world resists all of our fantasies of success and control, have a great deal to teach us.

And poetry, surely, is the same.

When my basketball career was nearing its end, I wrote this prose poem about what the game had meant to me.

COMPETITION AND FATIGUE, OR BASKETBALL

When I came downstairs the back door was standing open. We always lock it, at least my wife always locks it, but trying to be a good planetary citizen and save a few nickels I've stuffed the jamb so full of weatherstrip and foam that the latch will barely hold. I try to imagine the moment in the night when it let go, what little changes added up to enough.

I walk to faculty meeting on five hours of sleep. It's so cold the snow doesn't even cling to my shoes, the sky clear but pale, the houses closed off, sending only smoke to the sky. A few whiffs of oak among the flavorless gas, some kind of unconscious offering.

I'm sore and almost lightheaded from late-night basketball and the adrenalin that keeps me up for hours afterward. Again we lost, again I missed all my shots, again I yelled at the students trying to referee and was ashamed afterwards. I woke up at six-thirty still buzzing, making strategy for next time, trying to force myself back to sleep.

Yet I feel good, cleansed, as though failing at enough things guarantees some kind of triumph any day. I feel obscurely justified dressed in old sweats and shorts, each claiming a false allegiance, picked up secondhand on my way out of town. I run the court full of the best ideas, waste my breath dashing toward false hopes, keep thinking this time the surprise will be pleasant. I pant and fall down, trying to make miracles, and get up and insist I'm all right, and truly it doesn't hurt until later.

So I walk through cold, through fatigue I'm trying to believe is healthy, dreaming of an energy that will nudge my doors open while I sleep, dreaming of a language that will grasp and fix the shivery joy of walking over crusted snow, of swinging the door shut after a night of trying to heat the world, of leaving my family still warm in bed.

I cross the little creek. After a week of cold only the quickest water is still flowing, making a crooked little track through the ice and snow. The dark water gurgles quietly down a tiny slope, disappears, acting for all the world as if it knows how crazy it is to think of making anything happen, as if it knows that gravity and the shapes of earth are all we need to lean against and flow.

MY TWO OBSESSIONS

Basketball and Poetry

MARIAN HADDAD

JANUARY 16, 2007. I WOKE UP EARLY AND, OUT OF HABIT, SAT AT MY computer—entered nba.com into my search engine to check the news for the day, to ascertain which games were to be played between which teams and when.

Then I slid into espn.com, yahoosports.com, foxsports.com, si.com, and a number of other sports sites. All the while, ESPN played on my TV as I worked at my desk: SportsCenter, Cold Pizza/First Take, Skip Bayless, Mike and Mike, the gods of basketball-mania spending the day arguing about players and stats and fact and possibility. And then the subscription to NBATV. Sometimes I'd keep the sound off, but to this day, I maintain easy access: peripheral vision often wakes me out of a work stupor—Duncan—or the Spurs—or Garnett being interviewed—replays flashing across a screen. Multiple media outlets keep me plugged in. Sheer love for the game.

I read on nba.com, on my first cyber-stop for that morning, on this same date in 1962, Wilt Chamberlain scored the most points ever in an All Star game, 42—took 24 rebounds.

I then slid into my modus operandi: stream of consciousness: a path to a poem.

1962, my birth year.

Born on the twenty-fourth of a particular month.

I continued making the random connections. Before I knew it, I was typing, nonstop, a flurry of thoughts that had to do with and stemmed from basketball and race and internationalism, all based on NBA teams, players, stats. None of it possible without the 1966 NCAA championship team (Don Haskins' Texas Western Miners) and their improbable win over Adolf Rupp's heavily favored Kentucky Wildcats.

After the release of the movie *Glory Road,* which depicts the rise of that team, Haskins reiterated almost constantly that he played seven black players for no political or social reason, though everything we do or don't do is political, even without our intending it.

How proud it makes so many of us to know Haskins was inherently color blind only a short time after the Civil Rights Act. He never took credit for playing five black men and two black substitutes. He said he played the best of the best. "I wanted to win." And "The Bear" did just that.

So this is the story of the poem that found me that day, the way it felt as it simply spilled out of me. Me just a vessel to catch it all. But I know better than that. Part of the reason the poem came to me on this day is—the vessel was filled up.

The first draft found the poem, caught it; the piece was ready to come to fruition. Ten minutes went by quickly. I typed, without restraint, pulling from a store of saved-up, learned or lived facts. This unexpected flurry spread itself across seven pages. The title came last: "In Celebration of the Athlete We Call Beautiful: for James Naismith, Canada."

It reminded me of a story I once heard from my sister, whose second child was born after only fifteen minutes of hard labor. The birth of this poem felt that quick.

The gestation period, however, began in the spring of 2001, and Wilt Chamberlain and his stats which flashed that morning on nba.com simply triggered the labor. As soon as I willingly entered that cyber-world, carrying the names and numbers which make up the poem, the poem spread itself out among generations of players from both conferences, including numerous players from varied countries who now played in America.

This kind of love for and knowledge of a subject is bound to leap out of a poet. It surprises the poet, and yet the poet can see the expectedness of such a thing, due to living the subject somehow.

I had done some significant time loving and learning the game. I'm not being hyperbolic when I said I fell "headlong" into it.

For years, I had lived basketball daily, searched the basketball news of each day and the players who moved me. That morning, the poem simply— decided it was time.

When people asked how long it took, I'd answer, "Ten minutes?" That sounded ridiculous, even to me. They seemed stunned. "How could you know all those names, how to spell them? The foreign players? The stats?"

This is where revision comes in. I made the most recent revisions to the poem in July 2009.

For the first few weeks, which turned into months, I walked around my place quoting it. I literally could not fall asleep because the poem would not stop repeating itself in my head for months, maybe a year. Sometimes even to this day.

I called people and read it. Regularly. Repeatedly.

Self-aggrandizement? No.

Compulsion. Immersion.

The poem came out of that. It took me six-plus basketball seasons to accumulate the names, the numbers, the years, the countries—and for two-and-a-half additional seasons, I continued to revise it.

Of course, that poem was being written somewhere inside my subconscious. I lived poetry. I lived basketball. They lived together in one space—my head. The poem began to take notes inside me, began to write itself down.

The ten-minute draft was the easy part. Living with the poem and literally turning it over in my head and on the page was a different story. Reading it aloud, playing with line-lengths and breath and space; trying different routes into and out of it.

153

I thought it would be hard to find an audience for the poem. The majority of poets I knew didn't seem to be basketball fanatics. Some appreciated the game, but none were fanatics. And, of course, many basketball lovers I knew didn't attend poetry readings. Different sets of attractions. Occasionally I would get lucky, and the two groups would merge somehow.

Once, weeks after a reading, I was approached by an audience member who said, "Basketball is not on my radar, I'm sorry. When you started the poem, I had to leave. I heard all the poems you read before that, but when you introduced this as a *basketball* poem, I thought that'd be a good exit." She could not fathom a serious poem being about the sport.

Occasionally, there will be a man who scurries up to me after a reading, surprised and seemingly enthusiastic. One recently shared, "I'm not a fan of poetry, but I lovvvve that poem!" He shook my hand profusely, for minutes; it seemed as if he felt somehow infused or, maybe, enlightened about *poetry*, even telling me that he'd made the leap into it that night—and he had.

I feel this same pleasure in the poem when it takes a poetry lover or critic by surprise; their eyes gain focus and interest as the reading of the piece continues. At the end of the poem, they come up and say, "That's not only about basketball, you know. That's about race and internationalism and politics and art and the body and passion and resilience. It's not only about basketball! It's really good." I just smile, because—even if it were only about basketball, that would be fine, too. The gift of the extended metaphor carries that poem, reminding us of its effectiveness.

Basketball becomes, then, the springboard, for everything else in the piece. And two incredibly divergent groups of people end up connecting in a way they may not have before—sitting in the same room with a poet uniting basketball "and" poetry.

Each group I refer to in that audience ends up finding the other, and finding poetry in an unexpected subject—making the discovery that basketball *is* important "enough," in and of itself, to carry—a poem.

Up until my graduate school years, I attended very few UTEP Miners games while living in my native city of El Paso, Texas, most often on the occasional date with men who were addicted to hoops. All I understood then was the free-throw line and points made while players stood almost-still behind the line. My interest was still not tapped.

It was not until I took a job as an academic tutor for some of the athletes at San Diego State during my graduate school years in the late 1990s that my interest was caught. And when my interest is "caught" and "tapped" *in anything,* I become deeply involved in the subject at hand.

I recall being urged by a supervisor in the tutorial department to attend some football and basketball games. Anyone who has been a graduate student, carrying full loads during each semester, holding a full-time job and three part-time jobs, knows the last thing a graduate student has time for is attending games, particularly if we have not yet become, ourselves, addicted to these sports or even slightly engaged in them. I made it through football season without attending. Though I would have loved to, the schedule did not allow. It was around March, and the basketball season was at its height, when I was gently reminded that I had not yet once supported any of the athletes by attending their home games, and it might be a good idea for me to make the next Aztec basketball game, and, "Oh, by the way, here are two tickets."

I muttered all the way to my car, thinking I had no time for such things. Having already given up sleep and much of my social life, how in the world was I going to add this "game" to my list of things to do when I was already under inordinate stress and pressing deadlines? Mutter to myself, mutter to myself, but I had to go. "I should *at least* attend this one, just to be supportive," I thought out loud, "even if I have to pull an all-nighter when I come home."

So, the day came. I did not use my extra ticket to ask a friend: I had barely been able to *make* the game, last minute. So, I trudged up the steps of the gym, midway, arriving about half an hour before tip-off. I brought loads of papers to grade, as I was also a tutorial assistant for some rhetoric and composition classes, and figured, "I'll grade papers during this time." I was there only "in body" and gesture.

I became immersed in grading for half an hour or so until start time. Even after the tip I continued to try to grade, despite the cheering, the bottoms of shoes squeaking up and down wooden floors, and blaring time clocks. Occasionally, I'd look up.

I don't know exactly when, during the game, it happened—but it happened, and there was no looking back. It was like falling in love, being struck by lightning, being anointed with clarity of vision, and my addiction to the beauty of basketball began.

The Aztecs were playing the Utah Utes. And at that one point when I happened to look up, I saw something more beautiful than I'd ever seen in *any* sport (a dance of sorts), something I have yet to see, in that exactitude, again; that same ball movement has never yet been replicated in any of the multitudinous college and NBA games I have watched since then. There have been moments that have come close to that metronomic passing, but no cigar. That one moment, that semicircle of a dance—had become my moment of epiphany.

There were the Utes, in their crimson jerseys, forming a horseshoe of sorts, seemingly playing some version of keep-away, and in my mind, all I could see was this incredible metronome-like rhythm, and at the same time, the fluid movement known as "passing the ball." It was a dance. That one game—I recall the semicircle of men, keeping the ball in the air, in that half arc, ball shifting from hand to hand. I was stunned. I could not take my eyes off the game again. It was clear to me: This was art.

It makes sense to bring the two together. Basketball and poetry. It seemed and still seems clear to me that the Utes and their ball movement on that day I came to love the game, emulated metronomic movement; the passing of the ball, that day, became, for me, a dance, a kind of poetry. To this day, I have yet to see that almost-accidental perfect rhythm; the ball being "kept away in air," and the different touches it finds as it is volleyed from player to player, mimetic of dance; watching the ball, then, becomes to a degree, hypnotic.

Something else that feels dance-like, but less fluid, more pronounced, movement-specific and sharp in its execution, is the pump fake; particularly when Duncan executes it. Equally important, more important, perhaps, is the fact that when Duncan or any player pump-fakes, he "buys time"; he uses "white space" to manipulate the response of the defender. Poets use white space like that, whether it be the use of enjambment and lineation, whether it be the use of isochronic space (referred to as isochrony) creating white space within a line, space for breathing—what a photographer or visual artist might call negative space. When an isochronic break or line break is used, for me—it's synonymous with a pump fake.

Poets manipulate the reader's eye and the poem's pacing whenever they break or start a line, whenever they use stanzaic form over stichic, even when they use a period, a comma, a dash, a semicolon. Punctuation becomes one of the most effective tools to speed or slow the reader's eye and the poem's breath. We, as part of our art, do what composers do—decide where that breath should occur for highest impact. Whenever I see that pump fake, I think, line break. Stop. Restart. The executor of said movement, whether player or poet, then, controls the result.

Another way poets control their result is to choose line lengths. Short Creeley-esque lines create freeze-frames—sometimes, a staccato rhythm. They slow the reader and the poem down. The longer a line move—say a midlength line—we lose some of that staccato, some of that freeze-frame effect; we gain, instead, a more fluid line, the line moves faster, more smoothly, the more space it is given to stretch.

A much longer line spreads itself across much or most of a page—creates a mellifluousness that the midlength line does not, and is then, antithetical in a way, to the short staccato freeze-framer. Is one better than the other? They all serve their purpose; it becomes the poet's choice as to which line length suits each poem at hand, line by line, stanza by stanza, until the entire poem has found its form.

The trajectory the ball is given during varied shots somehow feels the same as varied line lengths. For instance, a slam dunk feels staccato. The more quickly and deliberately and powerfully the ball is dunked, the more staccato it seems, but the drive to the basket and the windmill arm movement or however the player chooses to execute the throw-down, carries that staccato to a higher degree. The "slammier" the dunk gets, the more profoundly that moment is punctuated—the sassier it is.

A midrange shot *is* more fluid in its flight, less punctuated, smoother in its delivery, carries an airiness—a lighter quality.

Finally, the popular shot made "from downtown," from "behind the arc," the Bruce Bowen corner three—the Finley three after three after three—or the Nowitski flight, the beautiful trajectory from the furthest space on the court, to the basket. Though Dirk's threes feel much more *Nutcracker Suite* and floaty, and the arc on the ball is graceful—juxtapose that to the zoom-lens, lethal, faraway shot that feels like a bull's-eye when Ray Allen shoots and makes. Or the accidental half-court or three-quarter-court desperation three that goes in, sent from a courageous Sheed. Variations on a theme; some seem "nailed," while some seem as if they are extended and leaping, the higher the arc, as if in a ballet, until the net is reached (see Nowitski).

The way the poet chooses to execute an entire poem—say, a poem that does not carry stanzas but one firm extended body versus the poem that is stanzaicly developed brings me to this. I have always felt the four quarters in basketball are a firm four-quatrain poem. Each quatrain stands by itself but gains resonance via the stitching to the following quatrain, until the poem (or game) is complete; reminiscent of the balance that comes from the four directions.

Say, the poet prefers to create a "movement," as in Beethoven's symphonies, then the first movement is not limited to the quatrain, the four lines—it could take up a whole page but might be marked I, II, III, IV or 1, 2, 3, 4 or as some poets have done, A, B, C, D, or merely using an ornament to separate the movements (§). Either way, whether a four-line formal or free-verse quatrain, whether a page-long movement, each carries what a quarter of a game carries—its own life, meaning, implications, and surprises.

But stitch the quarters together, and you have a whole story, a more expansive narrative. Of course, the overtimes are always surprises; any poem needing more space and flow can then create the additional quatrain or movement. And a book is an even longer stitching, not of quatrains or tercets, but of whole poems that speak to each other, a final collection, an entire season.

Now, the surprise at the end of a poem should almost always feel as intense, as unexpected, as a last-second, game-changing shot. Of course, we have the more fluid and expected endings, which also work, the 20-point game lead with 1.7 seconds left. We know the team leading will win, though we don't know by how much. Whether the ending is an entire surprise or more anticipated—it should always be effective.

Remember Larry Bird, '87 Celtics? Eastern Conference Finals. The series was tied 3–3. It seemed the Pistons were going to take the game and the series. The game was winding down; the Pistons were feeling confident. Isaiah inbounds a pass, Bird steals and passes to Dennis Johnson for the winning layup. The Celts were going to the NBA Finals!

Surprise endings tear the rafters down—what a surprise ending does in a poem. It creates a shaft of wind up the back of the neck, as opposed to a peaceful fadeout, which also has its place.

Closer to home for me—Derek Fisher, Game 5, 2003–2004 NBA Western Conference Semifinals, the series was tied 2–2. Last-minute heroics by Kobe took the Lakers up by a point, then Duncan makes a desperation fade away eighteen-footer with Shaq on the double-team defense. Duncan's shot goes in! Spurs 73. Lakers 72.

0.4 seconds on the clock; none other than Fisher shoots and makes, a tenth of a contested second left. Lakers ended up taking Game 5 and the series, 4–2, as the Spurs were ousted from the postseason, losing the opportunity for back-to-back league championships. Surprise endings, clearly, have impact beyond measure and beyond forgetting.

Finally, the escape or the entry? Oftentimes, I enter both poetry and basketball for either: amplified entry into reality (postseason), or an escape from reality (regular season). There is nothing more healing and hypnotic to me than watching the back-and-forth of a game on hardwood after a hard day's work, losing the day in the muscular overtures of Michael Finley, the grace, the leap, the movement; keeping our eyes on the ball can be hypnotic, addictive—one of many reasons, I cannot lose this game.

FOURTH QUARTER

"MORE BEAUTIFUL THAN WORDS CAN TELL"

A Poet's Education in Southern Basketball

BOBBY C. ROGERS

Language struggles with depicting physical action . . .

—*THE CRAFTSMAN,* RICHARD SENNET

BY MIDSEASON, THEY'VE FINALLY FIGURED OUT THE THREE-MAN weave. The slap of the ball against the gym floor obliterates the grind of city traffic outside and comes close to erasing the scream of cargo jets settling toward the FedEx hub for the evening sort. I'm coaching my son's fifth- and sixth-grade basketball team. They're all fifth-graders, and a few fourth-graders "playing up"—we haven't been winning much—and, what's worse for them, they have a poet for a coach. But I'm also an old varsity basketball player who had the game branded on his consciousness at a young age, and no matter how hard I've tried to unlearn everything that was yelled at me in the high school gymnasiums of West Tennessee, I still carry it all, what Whitman would call "my old delicious burdens," a pile of knowledge, not much good to me now, that won't be got rid of.

They finish the drill and look at me to see what we're doing next. What is it I'm trying to pass on to these kids? What do I want them to learn from this game? My own relationship to basketball is fraught and haunted, a history of struggle veined with disappointment, and what may as well be called heartache, and only the rare moment of transcendence—which just as precisely describes my relationship to poetry. My playing days were a long time ago, miles from here, in the smallest of Tennessee towns. Now I live in Memphis, a city that produces McDonald's All-Americans and NBA lottery picks. John Calipari and Mike Krzyzewski wander into prep school practices. If my kids ever wear a varsity jersey in this town, they'll need to have a lot more game than their daddy ever did.

In Carroll County, Tennessee, where I grew up, we played all the sports we had. Baseball in the summers on Little League teams with names like KECO Milling and Brown Shoe Company, tackle football games in a neighbor's sideyard while a transistor radio broadcast John Ward's play-by-play from Neyland Stadium, and then the retreat indoors for basketball once the weather turned. But basketball was the game that most transcended its season—no matter the month, it was hard for us to walk past a rim without putting up a few shots, waiting to see if anyone heard the bouncing ball and might come join in a game of Twenty-one. We all had the *Sports Illustrated* cover with University of Tennessee stars Ernie Grunfeld and Bernard King smiling for the camera taped to the wall in our bedroom. Such a clutter of images I can still call up. The man in the wheelchair who was allowed to sell chewing gum over by the trophy case. The cheerleaders along the baseline in their saddle oxfords trying not to look bored. The smell of popcorn, always the smell of popcorn. The Tennessee Secondary School Athletic Association had outlawed ice in cups, so a Coke had to be downed fast before it went warm and flat in the sultry gyms. High in the far wall, a dust-grayed vent fan straining to keep the air breathable.

Sports in a small southern town was where I had my early lessons in excellence. There were no poets or sculptors to model a life on, no one toiling away on a novel, and, in a farming and light manufacturing community of 5,000 people, not that many professionals of any stripe. But the dinner banquettes and church pews were full of folks who had done something of note on the football field or in the baseball state playoffs. The young know what excellence is. I was already finding it in the pages of Camus and Hemingway and Frost, Eliot's "Preludes," a few anthologized Dickinson poems, my first lines of Whitman. And Bernard King and Ernie Grunfeld. In the Zen-less world of a West Tennessee small town, you find your masters where you can.

The most essential things I know about form, I learned on the basketball court. A fast break has many components to be timed and crescendoed in just the right rhythm. So does a jump shot. Every artistic act is composed of parts and the joining of them into some coherent relationship. You can't run a rudimentary drill in practice without having the pieces fit at least clumsily together. A poem is as boundaried and rule-driven as any basketball game. Even a poem that flaunts its openness—Whitman's "Poem of the Open Road," say—is funneled and directed by its rules and repetitions. The road metaphor is more controlling than any syllable-logic or rhyme scheme, and the poem still must play out across a finite page, according to some implicit grammar. These forms test us: "Here is a man tallied—he realizes here what he has in him, / the past, the future, majesty, love—if they are vacant of you, you are vacant of them."

The uninitiated complain that basketball is the same thing over and over, back and forth from rim to rim. I'll admit, there's something to it. In the NBA, most offensive possessions don't even involve the running of a designed play. Every trip down the court is a variation on the one before it, and the one before that, arcing back ultimately to Dr. Naismith's gym with the peach baskets nailed to the wall. But they are no more the same than every line of Whitman is the same, than every day of our lives is the same. You don't have to read very far in the Psalms or in *Leaves of Grass* to taste just how rich repetition and variation can be:

> The earth never tires,
> The earth is rude, silent, incomprehensible at first, nature is
> rude and incomprehensible at first,

Be not discouraged, keep on, there are divine things well
envelop'd,
I swear to you there are divine things more beautiful than
words can tell.

Practice is rhyme and meter; the game is free verse (unless you're running the Princeton offense). I remember pieces of practices and meaningless JV games as vividly as I recall the varsity contests of the one season I was a starter and the gym was bright and loud. No explaining it. Even games of H-O-R-S-E and Around the World played on a backyard goal with a cheap fiberglass backboard and faded red, white, and blue net have found a way to lodge in my memory. Everything southern tends to devolve into story and raw image, as garish as a William Eggleston photograph. During a rebounding drill a sophomore guard took a fake and then got caught under the jaw with a shoulder on the way back down. His incisors landed on the court between my feet with a delicate sound like two Tic-Tacs dropped on a coffee table, perfectly clean and bloodless, their roots long and white. My father was watching practice that day. He came down out of the bleachers and said, "Pick 'em up, put 'em in your mouth. I'll drive you to the doctor's office." We resumed the drill.

The game had something to teach me about rejection. And I'm not just talking about all my shots that got blocked. I had made the junior high basketball squad in the seventh grade. I never got on the court when it mattered, but I came to enjoy the practices, the echoing acoustics of an empty gym, afternoons running with my friends, the sound of shoes barking each time we made a cut. I had a bad feeling, though, as tryouts were drawing to a close during the fall of my eighth-grade year. Like anyone else, I've experienced the usual run of rejections, both personal and professional, and like any writer I've been rejected countless times with tiny rejection slips, with editors' hardly decipherable handwritten notes, with no response at all. But I will say it has never gotten worse than that morning in the hallway of the old junior high school when the team roster was posted. The typed list had been tacked to the corkboard outside the principal's office, coats were rowed on hooks along the walls and crowds of students were pushing past, the dusty smell off the radiators was enough to make you choke, reading through the list as fast as I could, two times, three times, then turning and walking away, trying to appear as though I hadn't had any interest in it at all. In truth, trying to disappear.

I kept playing the game. Our eighth-grade science teacher decided to work with the kids who hadn't made the team. The rejects, the scrubs. He'd been a famous shooting guard at the tiny Cumberland Presbyterian College in town. There was an uncoordinated kid already over six feet tall he was taking on as a project; I was just along for the ride. We got to suit up for the last game, wearing vintage uniforms cut from some kind of shiny material that didn't match the rest of the team. His work with the tall kid didn't pan out, but I learned to shoot a basketball.

The next year, playing on the high school team didn't even cross my mind, but I made it to the finals of the school H-O-R-S-E competition which were held as a sideshow during the pep rally assembly for the homecoming football game. A senior was beating me "R" to "O" when time elapsed, and I hadn't even gotten to use my falling-out-of-bounds baseline around-the-edge-of-the-backboard jump shot I could always count on for a letter. A friend talked me into going out for the team. It was all a lark. The high school coach would let just about any freshman run with the team, but you had to earn a uniform. No freshman was dressing out that year. Around midseason we had a snowstorm that shut down school—it doesn't take much in Tennessee—but nothing shut down basketball practice. I showed up every day to do drills, play scout team when needed, run suicides with the starters. During those snow days one of the players was kicked off or quit, it was never clear which, and a uniform became available. A senior forward spoke up, "He's doing the work, Coach. Give it to him." And, quick as a backdoor cut, I was dressing on the varsity.

To dedicate years of practice to something as contrived and limitation-exposing as basketball will ruin you for all half-assed endeavor. As poor an athlete as I was, I have a disdain for hobbyists to this day. Any accomplishment worth talking about should exact some pain from you, some sacrifice measurable in years. I've never learned to trust what comes easy. My wife laughs at the low opinion I hold of the kids playing ultimate Frisbee in the green space across the street. It takes 10,000 hours to learn how to shoot a basketball, to be able to do it under pressure, in the fourth quarter, poorly. With a Frisbee, it takes until you get the thing out of the shrink wrap. My senior year, when I had started our season opener against the team from the county seat, jumped center, scored 10 points, hauled in a few rebounds, fouled out late in the fourth quarter when we already had the game won (I never saw the sense in leaving unspent fouls out on the court), the science teacher who had worked with the eighth-grade losers—he was now assistant coach of the girls team—came over to where I sat in the locker room still in my uniform, and, as if I were watching a made-for-TV movie, I knew what he was going to say before he said it: "Not bad for a junior high reject."

We were not an especially good team (our record was 15–10) in a not especially good league (Class Single-A, the smallest high schools in the state), but playing basketball took me out of my interior world of reading and dreaming, and thrust me into a world of hard facts. The bus rides through Trezevant and Atwood and Milan and Medina during the dark months of the year, finally arriving outside a harshly lit gym, were real in a way that reading "The Snows of Kilimanjaro" wasn't. It was not a perfect world. Tennessee may have been the last state to allow its high school girls teams to run full court. Until 1980, the girls game was played according to six-on-six half-court rules, supposedly more suited to their delicate physiognomies. Even then I thought it strange and demeaning: a three-on-three game at each end of the court, the defenders dribbling to the center line to hand the ball off to the offensive unit. The players on the defensive end wouldn't take a shot the entire season, maybe not during their entire career: playing guard was literal. The year before the TSSAA saw fit to switch to full court for girls (a little late considering Tennessee had produced Pat Head Summit, and the Lady Vols were already hanging national title banners in Knoxville), the freshmen boys scrimmaged against the varsity girls team, doing our best to bring them into modernity, and I will attest that some of their physiognomies were less delicate than others, especially when I was in the paint trying to get a rebound. Here's where I first became aware of structural sexism. The girls game had, in effect, been halved so the players wouldn't be required to master so many skills, the court was halved so they wouldn't be called on to exert themselves so much.

Basketball brought home other realities. Our town and team were integrated, but not all the farming communities in that end of the state were so cosmopolitan. After winning a close game (actually, it wasn't that close) at one particular town up near the Kentucky line, we had to leave the court through a shower of popcorn and paper cups and racist epithets. It suddenly became clear to me why ice had been outlawed. Our coach knew the signs better than we did. "Forget the showers," he said, "Let's get the hell out of here." He was an elder in the Church of Christ and only used strong language when he'd exhausted every other remedy. We got the hell out of there.

Like most sport's careers, mine ended with a loss. We had barely survived the district tournament, and in the first round of the regional we got beat by 20. In the locker room after the game, the coach began chatting with the returning players about getting ready for next season. I was a senior, there was no next season. In my callowness, I had been ready to leave every piece of high school behind for weeks now, longing to watch every petty vestige of small-town life getting smaller in the rearview mirror as I drove out of there to college and whatever came next. Everything but this. The #14 jersey went into the pile on the floor for the managers to gather up, launder, and put away for next year.

To makers of metaphor, basketball is as good a vehicle as any, I guess, as good as Whitman's open road: "You express me better than I can express myself, / You shall be more to me than my poem." When I did depart my hometown, the game went with me. I couldn't leave it on the locker room floor. In Jackson, Tennessee, in Knoxville, in Charlottesville, Virginia, there were always courts with players standing on the sidelines needing one more body before they could say "We got next." A pickup game is usually played among strangers, but basketball is the Latin of the playground. If the ball comes out the bottom of the net—whether the net's made of clean white nylon or chain links or not even there—the basket counts. I played a lot of pickup games, intramural games, or just shot a few baskets by myself. On one of those campuses, I learned what a trope was and might have said Whitman's desire "To know the universe itself as a road, as many roads, as roads for traveling souls" could for some of us be an open court, a run-out on a fast break, filling a lane, receiving the pass and getting the ball up on the iron.

I had the honor to play basketball with the poet Tom Andrews when we were students in Charlottesville. He was in the class ahead of me, a few years older, immeasurably wiser, a better writer, a better person. Before he died in the summer of 2001 at the age of forty, he'd written two collections of poetry and a memoir about his life as a motorcycle-riding, risk-taking hemophiliac. (Tom died of a blood disease unrelated to his hemophilia and, so far as I know, unrelated to basketball.) He's been well elegized— notably by Charles Wright in the title poem of his 2005 book *Buffalo Yoga* and in Don Platt's Pushcart-selected "Brother Death, Sister Life." Saturday mornings in Memorial Gym, we'd get together to play some one-on-one or maybe find a pickup game. I never understood how someone who couldn't pass a physical to participate in varsity sports had become such a fundamentally perfect ballplayer. Who knows what drove him? For a guy who bled, he played a hard-nosed game. In his work as well as his living, Tom seemed to love the jostlings between the reposed abstractions of high art and the random violences of the world. Basketball, the way I played it, was full of random violences. It was probably during our first workout that he told me he was a hemophiliac. My skills were not necessarily suited to a finesse game, but suddenly that's how I played. Tom had courage. If he turned an ankle he would be on crutches for a week or more. When we left the court, I was just glad I hadn't killed him.

I'll elegize him this way. Once Tom and another poet Loren Graham and I were shooting around when the SAE fraternity team came in and challenged us to a game. The gym was empty; we were all they had to practice against. They gave us their worst guy, which was fine, we weren't going to pass to him anyway, and someone shot to see who got ball first. Loren, who didn't have the greatest mobility because of an old foot injury, was tall enough and mean enough to clear the boards, Tom was the quickest guy in the gym, taking the outlet pass and streaking down the court, and I had been taught how to fill a lane. They never found a way to defend us. At some point, one of the players on the fraternity team asked, "So what do you guys do?" It was clear from our appearance we weren't traditional undergraduates. And, just standing around, we didn't look much like ball-players. "We're poets," Tom said.

The more you've played the game, the more it ceases to be a metaphor for anything. A couple of years ago, I was at the Mason Y out by the University of Memphis, sitting in the bleachers while Coach Tiffany, who played at local powerhouse White Station High School before her college career, put my son and daughter and a dozen other kids through their paces, teaching them the difference between "deny" defense and "help" defense (man-to-man concepts get taught early around here). Their first basketball clinic. A garbage can was stationed on the court to catch water from a leaky roof, but everyone just played around it. During the drills they all had smiles on their faces, and during the instruction they looked up at the coach with a solemn intensity. The bouncing of the balls, the kids' feet on the hardwood, the sound of the rain on the roof on a Saturday morning—I wish I knew what the game would bring them. Maybe an instance or two of friendship, an understanding of what's below the surface of any accomplishment, maybe to become

> Journeyers over consecutive seasons, over the years, the curious years
>   each emerging from that which preceded it,
> Journeyers as with companions. . . .

On the way home from the district tournament at Greenfield my junior year in high school, the team bus broke down. The world is dark out in the country, a half a dozen miles from a streetlight. Back then I was used to it. The driver turned on the dim emergency flashers and got out to throw up the hood of the old yellow bus. Before we had time enough to wonder what was going to happen, sedans and station wagons began pulling over, parents and neighbors seeing if there was anything they could do. We piled into the backseats of the cars and made a caravan back to town, ahead of us a row of taillights to mark the bendings in the narrow highway that took us home.

BLESSED

ROSS GAY

1.

I have been blessed by elbows. Elbows intentional and elbows incidental. Elbows brought forth in the fury of a rebounding scrum, and elbows caught flush from a seven-footer's drop step. Elbows planted with eyes firmly set on their target and elbows flailing off balance until the face or shoulder or neck stopped its fall. Elbows fleshy and elbows sharp as swords. Elbows like tree trunks to leave a crick in your neck for weeks and ninja elbows that open your face without you knowing it. Yes, I have been blessed by elbows.

And I have been blessed by teachers in the art of elbows. Among the best teachers were a couple of former pros, well into their forties, whose science was meticulous and precise, looming and painful. These men (whose names here will be withheld lest this essay fall into the wrong hands and some long-burning animosity get stoked before a reunion game) had mastered their practice, I gather, as slightly undersized, or underathletic fighters in the 1970s pro game, playing in the midst of folks like Kareem Abdul-Jabbar and Dave DeBusschere and Bob Lanier, all of whom, I would guess, might not so difficultly rumple your chest into the flimsy sack of feathers it really was unless you let it be known quickly, I would guess, that the hinges moving those arms about, that gave that baby hook or twelve-foot jumper its sweet and gentle touch, were also bones, and thick, and harder than a face. Whether you're one of the best players of all time or not.

And in the slower games of these men in their forties—games slower than before, but still quick and hard, a hell of a lot smarter than any kids' game, as you can tell when a gang of fit older guys who can play run a bunch of kangaroos who can't set a back pick, much less run off one; older guys who know that if everyone crashes the offensive glass well sure enough they're gonna' leak out their guard and score at least half their points on uncontested fast breaks, and sitting the kangaroos on the sideline—the elbows were quiet and ever-present. They might emerge beneath your chin as someone jumped for the rebound you jumped too early for, your plummet meeting their ascent—pray your tongue's in your mouth and you don't already have a toothache.

They might show up in a basic post move: catch the ball on the block, ball secured beneath the chin and elbows already flaring (nothing like a butterfly's grace unless a butterfly was made of two-by-fours . . .), slight fake baseline to get you leaning, because you know your young legs, your kangaroo legs, twenty years younger than this old-timer, this used-to-been, this rickety giant five inches your senior but much more than that your slower, the tape at his knees fraying, his shorts a bit too short and shirt not quite long enough to meet his waistline, socks up high, the same one who will spend a full half hour after the workout stretching, doing sun-salutations and side bends, groaning like a bull each time he folds over to touch his toes, who needs a half hour to warm up—jumping jacks, laps around the court, alternate toe-touches—to be sure his hamstrings don't explode, to make sure his brittle Achilles tendons don't disintegrate, to get "the blood flowing," as he says, to get "these old bones moving," and because you're quick you lean six inches instead of the half he needs, and he spins middle so fast you don't even see the elbow denting the back of your neck, though when you catch your balance you feel it and wonder where the bat went.

And there's another way the elbow from the masters would make itself known. And though elegant is the word that comes into my head over and over again, I don't quite know if that's right. Perhaps there's an elegance to brute honesty, and this is what I'm landing on. Perhaps there's an elegance to the indiscreet warning that an elbow can offer. To the clarity of intent. Because there is clarity of intent when one saunters over to set a perimeter ball screen on a post man and that post man in no uncertain terms lifts up his shiny axe to the height of your mouth or throat and it would be a muffled singing you'd make if he buried it in you. If you set the pick the way you thought you were going to, that is. Which is to say you don't, and he'll squeeze through that screen just fine. And you'll both play another day.

Mind you, I came upon these teachers as a kind of lesser practitioner myself, having opened my fair share of faces on the way to the basket or settling into the post, or, if need be, if need be, and for other reasons. But with no such mastery and cleanliness, no such *grace*, as these men, one of whom, a former New York Knick, died on the very basketball court on which I was lucky enough to study with him briefly (died hauling in a rebound with his bows surely flared), the other of whom I heard, at sixty, is still banging around pretty good, and was just a couple of years ago still knocking down midrange jump shots in his 1970s shoulder heave that, along with those elbows, made him a second-round draft pick for the Milwaukee Bucks. Still, I'm sure, planting elbows in chests in the Lehigh Valley. Yes, part of what these men taught me, which I did not know about the elbow, was its grace, its discreet compulsion, its gentle teeter on the precipice of fair and fight. If you were to introduce a referee to the games played by the masters (but why would you, when you could call your own?), you would be hard-pressed to get a foul called in your favor. And still, you'd leave the game as bruised and busted as some more monstrous hooligan might leave you—the same hooligan who'd be fouled out in a reffed game, or come to blows on the street. Yes, I had elbows, and I used them to some effect, but it was this masterful and silent tutelage that opened another door. And in the days since and while studying with them, I have become nothing like a master, nothing of the sort, but let us say, proficient. (And let us also say that there is no small coincidence in the inverse relation of my increasing elbowic precision and decreasing grease in the joints of my lower body.) And let us say, also, that neither of these men was the best teacher I've had.

2.

The drill goes like this: A line of children at the corner of the court, on the baseline, where they receive a pass, give a pump fake to get the invisible man in the air, and get to the rim in one dribble. It's easy enough, especially for the bigger kids and the kids who have some kind of handle. A hard fake, one dribble, attack the rim—though if you don't dunk, you had better use the backboard, or there's a good chance the head coach will put your ass in a sling. Of course we make the drill harder for them—I make the drill harder for them—by standing on the box and tossing each one of their shots. Wap. Wap. Wap. Even the taller kids, the kids who might otherwise be dunking in this drill, can't quite figure out what to do with someone who jumps as high as them, is stronger than they are, and has the privilege of knowing exactly what they're trying to do. Wap to Andre. Wap to Charles. Wap to Scott. Maybe someone avoids the block by tossing up some garbage. Wap to Brandon. And here comes our little sophomore point guard, maybe two hairs on his chin, eeking his way, by now, into the starting rotation—a good enough player, smart about the game, willing to shoot tough shots and willing to give them up for better ones. But a sophomore, with maybe two hairs on his chin, who stands about 5'9". Because this kid is confident, and good, and has a certain kind of smile after he does something right, and a bit of a bounce in his step, *and I am, after all, his coach, his teacher,* I load up to block this thing so hard his ancestors will moan. *Maybe two hairs on his chin.*

It's strange to think that it all happened in an instant—probably less than three seconds. That Rodney caught the ball with his feet snuggled between the three-point line and sideline, threw a fake, pushed out one hard dribble, elevated off his right leg from a foot or so outside of the lane, twisted his body so that his shoulder would protect the ball, which he shifted from his right hand to his left, gathered enough torque in his waist and abdomen so

that his uncorked right elbow could explode full force into my mouth, looking first in the direction of my face—which was, in fact, moving through
the air as I went to block the shot—and then toward the rim, while main-
taining enough control of the ball that as he fell through the air, now almost
sideways, almost parallel with the ground, his feet slowly raising from his
elbow's stopped momentum, he was able to throw a shot toward the rim, a
shot that, in fact, hit the rim and barely rolled off, which he watched first
before taking stock of the small tornado he had become on my face, the
small lesson he had learnt me.

And there was another instant, during which Rodney lay half on his
back, half on his side, in the paint, holding his elbow, studying the small
lines of blood running down it from the tooth holes, and looking at me, my
face, which must have looked a little bit stunned (even though I was trying
hard to have a poker face), a little bit changed, which must have looked
at him differently than I had looked at him before, which must have made
him, too, see himself differently than he had seen himself before, holding
his elbow, his eyes between it and my face, during which the light in the
building changed just so.

Yes, while the masters of the elbow have shown me (and continue to
show me) the studied hacking at barriers to the basket or boards, the magical making of space, the subtle arrangement of the court as determined by
that rugged confluence of bones, Rodney's elbow moving through my teeth
was a reimagining of the world. Surely as he saw me come to block that
shot, just as I had blocked the fifteen shots before his (and his a couple times
before this as well), shots by bigger and stronger and more athletic kids sent
against the board or to the sideline, he must have imagined the fate of his
shot as well. And it was imagination that swung his elbow open like a door
into a world he had not yet seen. Yes, it was the elbow as an act of the imagination, as an invention of the world, as a kind of bold poetic line. Not the
elbow of revenge or justice. Not the sophisticate's elbow, nor the old-timer's.
Not the thug's elbow, nor the flail's. Nothing nasty or cheap, nothing dirty
or down-low. This was the elbow as visionary. Elbow as possibility. Elbow
as dream.

And with two of my lower teeth knocked almost clean out, squirming beneath my tongue, clinging by a couple threads of gum, while the drills went on, and I snuck into the locker room to wedge the things back where they belong, and called my friend the dentist, and ate gingerly for two weeks, and to this day have a slight numbness in that region of my mouth thanks to that little motherfucker's elbow, elbow that said to me, and so, to himself, *Here's how my story goes.*

IT WAS EASIER TO SAY, "I'M A BASKETBALL PLAYER" THAN IT IS TO SAY, "I'M A POET"

JACK RIDL

"How'd it go out there today? Did you work on your left hand? Shoot fifty free throws? Tap a hundred off the backboard? Work the key?" Those were the words I'd hear, often hear, daily hear from my father. He was a basketball coach. I was the coach's kid. I practiced. I practiced a lot.

My father was infinitely patient. I really wasn't that good. But how I worked. And how I imagined. The clock was always ticking as I took jump shot after jump shot at the hoop fastened to the back of the garage. The "court" was assembled from five-by-five squares of poured concrete, the cracks about a quarter of an inch between each slab. I knew without looking down where they lurked and could dribble left/right/back/left without hitting one. When I stepped to the foul line, time had run out, we were behind by a point, and I was shooting a one-and-one. When tapping the

179

ball off the board, I backed my opponent out and stood my ground. And along the sidelines, the fans were cheering or booing, and the cheerleaders were screaming and pushing back their long hair.

It wasn't until my dreams of playing the point for my father and taking his team to the Big Dance, the Final Four, the NCAA championship had faded along with my jump shot that I realized how much my imagination had kept me going. Like I said, I wasn't all that good, good enough for high school ball, starting from grade nine on, but never the star and never good enough to play in college and always all-but-terrified. It was my imagination that got me through. I could pretend. I could pretend that I was better than I was, pretend that the cheerleaders wanted to go with me to the dance after the game, pretend that one day I'd be at that foul line with the clock at zero and sink the winning two foul shots, pretend that one day I'd come back and everyone would point and whisper, "See that guy? He was the best guard this school has ever seen."

But poetry? When Curry Kirkpatrick, then of *Sports Illustrated,* wrote a piece about my father, he said to my dad, "Something that intrigues me is that your son is a poet. That's pretty weird, isn't it? A coach having a poet for a son?" I always wished that my father didn't have to be asked that question, that the question would have been, "How's it feel to have your son playing for the Celtics?"

In the late 1960s my father became the head basketball coach at the University of Pittsburgh. When I first thought the crazy thought that maybe I could write poems, I sought out poet Paul Zimmer to help me. He said he would. I had about fifty profoundly sensitive pieces, bad news from the heart. I showed him a couple. He said, very gently, "Let's start over." I asked Paul what he would charge for looking at my stuff. He said, "You know what I would really like? I'd love to be able to go to the Pitt locker room after games. Do you think that you could arrange that?"

I was floored. Ever since I was a child, I'd all but lived in the locker rooms of my father's teams. It was time to put away childish things, buy a cape and a pipe and be deep. Zimmer wanted to see the chalkboard and listen to postgame talks, watch the sports writers interview my father and the players, see guys celebrate or mope? This was definitely not deep. "Okay.

Sure," I said. Zimmer then added, "I have one little thing about the way I'll work with you: I'll tell you when I think you've written a poem." That was fine by me. I'd already spent about a year writing songs, trying to push Paul Simon off the charts, and I already had the fifty-some poems, even though Zimmer said we'd start over. This "one little thing" seemed only right to me. Why wouldn't he tell me if I'd written a poem?

Four years later, he told me I'd written a poem.

Several times I asked Paul if he thought I should quit. He always answered, "That's up to you. If you want to, you can." Why didn't I quit? I really think it was because I was and still am and always will be a coach's kid. You practice. For years, you practice. And you practice without ever knowing you'll get there. But you practice dreaming that you will.

And you take it from the coach. You take it and you take it and you take it. And you keep coming back. And you slam the locker door, and you curse the coach and the cosmos, and you stop. But you don't quit. You stop and wonder and doubt, and you think this is not only a waste of time but a waste of your life, and you think about all the people out there making money or having good times while you're staring at a lame image. You think you must be insane. And then you keep going because the word quit cannot ever become part of your life. Your jump shot may have faded, but you didn't quit. Your jump shot quit you.

And you learn not how to win but what to do when you lose. You never learn how to win. You just work the key and hit the boards and hope like hell and pick up the pen and listen to the words, the words, the words. And sometimes you feel that shake and bake, and the rhythms shake and bake, and the words fake left and go right, and you drive the lane and pull up or shoot a floater or break away for a slam dunk. And you get down and watch your opponent's belly and wait for that slipup and steal the ball and hit the open man.

Sometimes.

And when the mailbox brings another loss, you convince yourself that it was an upset and that you'll win the next one.

Today I practiced again. Tomorrow I'll practice again. The game never ends. The rhythms I learned on that backyard court are in me and in my language. The images are precise because there's so little room for error between ball and hoop, between ball and opponent's outstretched hand. And there is no such thing as getting it down, mastering it so you can do it all again the same way the next time. You can only prepare for the next game. You are always preparing for the next poem.

After I wrote the poem that Zimmer called a poem, he said, "You know you haven't learned to write poetry, don't you? You don't learn to write poetry. No one learns to write poetry. You always have to learn how to write the next poem." Practice.

READING SEBASTIAN MATTHEWS

JAMES MCKEAN

THE MINUTE I SAW THE BASKETBALL ON THE QUEEN'S UNIVERSITY campus in Charlotte, North Carolina, I should have made myself scarce. Then before I could decline, five of us were looking for a court, a game in the air like a good image in a poem suggesting possibilities. Electricity. A thought arcs, breaks and backdoors, reverses. My matchup, Sebastian Matthews, quotes his dad, saying a good pickup game demonstrates "that particular balance between pattern and improvisation." Is that what happened to us? With that "balance" in mind, I've been reading Sebastian's poems again. How his long lines in "I Got Next," from his book *We Generous,* pick up speed, running around the breaks, enjambing, stanzas in poem after poem full of moving screens. How the couplets in his "Working the Post with Jim McKean," published in *Ecotone,* feel like one-on-one quick riffs down the page. Every time I read this poem, I think of our pickup game that May afternoon, and how that old dog competition woke me up.

Our first day on campus, the ball was magnetic. Walking in the warm air of North Carolina, the magnolia blossoms huge, the humidity ascendant, I saw it a long way off, Sebastian's boy running on ahead, the ball an armful before he dribbled twice with both hands and fumbled the ball away, "After it," a basic principle he understood already.

My arms went lighter the closer he got. I flexed then cupped my hands. Sebastian wasn't even born yet when I started to play in college. I stopped playing organized basketball twenty-five years ago, and now in 2007 I still wanted the ball. "Here, here." I called in my mind, walking past, the future leaning over my shoulder, my right hand up waving to Sebastian. I was open all the way back to my room.

We had five days in Charlotte. The invitation sounded every time the ball thumped down the hall, on the sidewalk, beneath the magnolias. I drew the curtain aside to see. Whose idea was it to look for a basket? The ball's maybe, potential sewn into the leather, a can't-help-it, something tactile and visceral, until one day we lined up like filings to the magnet-ball, four poets and Geoff Becker the fiction writer. "We're just shooting around, right?" he asked. "My back's messed up."

"Sure," we said. The game's first misdirection.

We all knew where this was leading and I still wasn't sure I wanted to go there. There are always stakes, sore muscles and loss. What would I gain I hadn't gained years ago? My game has two sides: what I used to do—the head fake and drive after a fadeaway jumper—and what I only imagine now, my memory playing above the rim.

But I went, setting a screen on my own good sense, hoping my skills were only mothballed, pulled by something, needing a test maybe, my basketball game as obscure as a blank page. Someone had spotted a court in a neighboring schoolyard. We headed out, the day warm already, across the street from Queens, over a front lawn, around the classrooms toward a parking lot and there they were, two baskets with chain nets. *Magnets!* Now the factors of this equation were in place, except for quirks, how a cement curb ran parallel and directly beneath the bucket, a foot and a half in from the baseline technically. Odd and dangerous. Then there was the matter of permission, for as soon as we fanned out and lofted a few shots toward the rim, a young teacher who had been force-marching her grade-school kids single file around the yard, halted her charges close to the court and asked us who we were and without waiting for that answer said we couldn't play here.

She was maybe twenty-five, blue jeans, blue shirt, whistle around her neck, ponytail, walkie-talkie belted like a sidearm. We were five professors from five different schools in five different states. It was her yard. She yelled at one of her kids to stay out of the mud puddle. We saw what we were up against. We milled at the foul line, kicked dust up on the court, scanned the sky. One of us explained we were visiting teachers at Queens this week and thought we might shoot around some, just for a little while. Squinting, she said she needed to call this in and keyed her walkie-talkie, spoke, waited, looked up and said, "There's a red-tailed hawk in the neighborhood and a clutch of baby rabbits over by the building, getting picked off one by one." Then her walkie-talkie squawked, and she responded, "Yeah, I checked them out. They're okay."

She had traipsed her charges out to see a real contest, I thought, and now fibbed for the pretenders before her. She didn't know us. Maybe the ball gave us credibility, and permission granted, we thanked her. Someone shot. I rebounded and passed it out to Alan Michael Parker. He squared up at fifteen feet, released at the top of his jump and in the ball went. *He knows what's up.* Geoff heaved a set shot. Sebastian, a lefty, dribbled to my right, head down. *Shade that side.* Bob Hicok, who had said he doesn't play much b-ball, wandered and watched, ran the ball down when it rolled away, and dribbled back, watching the ball until he was too far under the basket. Sebastian backed in on no one, turned and threw up a fade-away jump shot. The ball went in and out. I rebounded and put it back off the board, wondering where my elevation had gone. Precise, Alan warmed up with purpose. Bob surveyed the court as if it were a set of plans. Geoff had second thoughts. I watched, rebounded, tried a short turnaround, and missed badly, the ball clanking off the rim.

Sebastian's poem says I'm "rusty." He is being kind. I had no timing and my muscles felt senile. But I felt the energy ratchet up, that competitive thing turning my head. Sebastian explains in "I Got Next" how b-ballers mill about the basket, "waiting to pass back made shots, dribbling out for an open look." And I remember watching him move left and right out the corner of my eye and see him again in his lines, "I'm cool, / though pure verve surges in me like sap. Itching to get my hands on / the ball, to break a fast sweat." Such energy. "It's an old feeling," he says.

Here's another feeling I had in Charlotte: *I'll stuff that sap of yours, Sebastian.* Now the dog inside me stirred. Sebastian backed in and I pushed back, easy at first and then harder, swiping at the air when he took a shot. Then someone said how about a game, and Geoff resigned right off, happy to kibitz. Then the remaining four of us paired off, Sebastian and Alan against me the old hand and Bob the rookie. And then we were at it.

Heavier, slower, and a head taller than Sebastian's lanky 6'3" frame, I figured the only way to mess with his frenetic in-and-out, up-and-down, left-and-right, blond-hair-bobbing basketball moves, was to get in the way. And I did. He passed back out or went too far under, tiptoeing the dangerous curb. I pushed. He shoved. I forearmed shivered. He stopped cold, reversed and went the other way. After five minutes, we were already out of breath. A break and then I had the ball, picked up my dribble, and looked for Bob. Having never played much basketball, he moved as if he always had, cutting toward the basket from every direction, this way that way, each move as unexpected as all the wacky phenomenal turns in his poems. He put his shoulder to Alan hard but just couldn't finish, a good move, a pass, and a layup too much to handle all at once. *A natural, he just needs practice.* Efficient, Alan rubbed Bob off on Sebastian's screens and drove the basket or pulled up for open jump shots, mixing his game up without waste, worked his sweet ironies into two points and the ball back.

Did we balance pattern and improvisation, Sebastian's father's recipe for a life well lived? We took break after break, I remember, sucking air and sweating, only Alan on his toes. There was nothing nostalgic about this game and no time to reflect. All centered on the moment, which meant zero analysis and my sincere effort to confound Sebastian Matthews, to deny him left or right, space, ball, basket, satisfaction, to take him inside, to get him off the ground, to keep him flat-footed, on my hip, away from the basket or underneath too far or out of range or off balance and hesitant or self-conscious or gun-shy, to keep him guessing, to let him understand too late that he had just been faked, juked, driven, stuffed, and denied. It's the desire to keep yourself on balance and your opposition off. Take that.

Some of it was easy. Bob entered the ball to me once at the low post, Sebastian pinned on my left hip; I dropped my right foot toward the basket, squared my body parallel to the backboard, kept him flailing on my back, the ball dribbled in front of me between my legs once, twice, then jumped up square and back into him, the ball laid up in front of me and a long ways out of his reach, neat and clean. I didn't jump much. Didn't have to. Sebastian responded with more contact, whacking at my arms. Good. It let me know where he was, and if I knew where he was and thought about going, I suggested he keep going that way, a leaning one way by design with the intent of going the other. The set up of a good joke. A good line in poetry. That sweet misdirection just when one expects the pattern to show. "Avoid the obvious" and "vary the avoidance," Robert Francis says.

When the ball found Sebastian, he was all movement, a loquaciousness of arms and legs and head fakes. But when he stuttered, dropped the left-hand dribble, picked up, I knew what was coming, filled in, a wall where he wanted to be, then swatted the ball away. It's as if he borrowed those moves, studied hard, adopted them, and gave me a pattern I could read. He generated the energy in our "slowed-down, / heat-drenched game of 2 on 2," a line from the good poem he wrote just for this game, for which I thank him, but must guard against. You see, the poem is fast and clever and at least in one little understated misdirection, wrong.

In my memory I'm still late, "off-balance" when he finally got me. What did I expect? I made the error of an assumption. Thought the same two dribbles meant his pulling up for a jumper. Thought I had him again, hands down, but he led me, faked, his right hand across his body turned into me, jumped, and tossed the jump hook, a lefty. Flat footed, I knew too late and watched the ball bounce a little at the bottom of the net, sweet even in the chains. I didn't see that one coming. Now I see it over and over. Now here in his poem I see him give that sweet move only half a line, the break after "show him" (that's right; let me commit), and the next line reading "my younger brother's lefty scoop." What? Sebastian gave the shot away, a shrug, the courtesy of attribution. Such modesty.

Sorry. I'm not buying that little shoulder fake. If that had been his brother's "scoop," I would have swatted it clear to Hoboken. That shot was all Sebastian's, jazzy, an instinctive riff, the improvisation when I expected the pattern. What he showed me wasn't what he did. Believe me. I wanted to strip him clean. But he took it to me and that made my game. I was back in the moment, awake, working hard, reading him close, as I do now, those good moves, a screen here and there, language that breaks, surprises, and rolls into points that are all his.

GOING EXACTLY WHERE
WE WANT TO GO

MARJORIE MADDOX

WHEN I WAS TEN, I DIDN'T NEED TO SEE A PHOTO TO KNOW THAT MY mother, a lanky beauty, had been an energetic and skilled basketball player, captain of her 1944, '45, and '46 high school team, the Clark Bars. The name itself intrigued me. Not only was it the favorite candy bar of my youth, but the reference to my mother's maiden name, Clark, confirmed in my young mind her indispensability! Ah, to have a team, any team, named after you!

In our family games, she seemed effortlessly to arc the ball high above the driveway, then—swoosh!—straight down through the waiting net. Meanwhile, my brother, sister, and I waded through such basketball farm-animal games as H-O-R-S-E and P-I-G.

It was the same with our other impromptu favorites—badminton, Ping Pong, croquet—which she often won with a clean swing or a perfectly aimed tap. It was not that I recognized her as an athlete; in the late 1960s and early 1970s, most moms were just considered, well, moms. What I caught in those jumps, turns, and throws was what she was before and without us. Her unassuming grace seemed easy and magical. I loved to watch her strong legs push off the asphalt, pivot just-so, and take her exactly where she wanted to go.

What I noticed most was how she loved having fun *with* us. This didn't mean she had to let us win—that went against her sense of fair play—but that she rejoiced in our shared experience of motion. In this way, whatever the final score, I felt as if I'd won. No matter that I wasn't and never would be an athlete. Despite lessons in tennis, roller skating, and dance, I never mastered the simple basics of coordination, instead, from an early age, practicing the motion and coordination of words. Through writing, I, too, could pivot just-so. I could go exactly where I wanted to go.

This simple delight in transporting oneself or an entire audience of readers from one court of the poem to another is what keeps players playing and writers writing. At the heart of game and poem is action. As athlete and author know, such action travels beyond physical boundaries. At its best, the play that emerges involves the whole being of each individual. On the court, the ball moves from one team member to another while, simultaneously, the individual and community of fans are "caught up" in the swell of rhythm and momentum. So, too, the poem. The writer passes, intercepts, and even occasionally slam-dunks images and ideas while, in delayed but similar motions, readers move in concert with poem and poet.

Although this emphasis on interconnectedness was one of my mother's many driveway basketball lessons, it reappeared in other childhood venues. The idea that we lived in community—be it as a member of a family, a class, or a team—was often in mind. Striving for personal best was not a contradiction; it was an outgrowth of living and working with others. Encouraging and respecting individuals became realistic components of competition. Such basics still float across my mind's court when I watch a double-team or a full-court press. The same happens when I read a line that expertly connects me to the poem. My first reaction is to cheer.

A similar interaction can and does happen in the act of teaching. In

"Patrick Ewing Takes a Foul Shot," a poem I often use in my Introduction to Poetry Writing class, Diane Ackerman uses powerful images and line/stanza breaks to build momentum. Even though the poet focuses on Ewing, the reader and the unmentioned team members are there in the game, watching each move.

> Ewing sweating,
> molding the ball
> with spidery hands,
> packing it, packing it,
> into a snowball's
> chance of a goal,
> rolling his shoulders
> through a silent earthquake,
> rocking from one foot
> to the other, sweating. . . .

We are *in* the poem because we are *on* the foul line. The action reoccurs every time we read these words. Ackerman's participles and her deliberate breaks set our minds' cameras on slow but almost-continuous motion.

> bouncing it, oh, sweet
> honey, molding it,
> packing it tight. . . .

At the stanza break, she holds us—and the ball—in suspension:

> he fires:
> [stanza break]

The lines of the poem expand the action of the game and the interaction with the poem's audience. We hang on each word the way we hang on the movement of the ball, waiting to see what will happen next, to what surprising or expected motion Ackerman will lead us. Will the words bounce out of bounds or soar straight through the net? With breath held, we wait for the next stanza—and the possible goal. Neither Ackerman nor Ewing disappoint.

> floats it up on one palm
> as if surfacing
> from the clear green Caribbean
> with a shell
> whose roar wraps around him,
> whose surf breaks
> deep into his arena
> where light and time
> and pupils jump
> because he jumps.

As a professor, I've watched students experience this poem. More often than not, they first recognize the poet's ability to capture the rhythm, motion, and magic of the familiar. Most of my students, like players admiring a skilled teammate, are inspired next to act. Through additional guidance and the strenuous practice of revision, I coach them to "go exactly where they want to go" in their individual work.

My first reading "coach," my mother, likewise inspired me through enthusiasm and example. While I could never have become an accomplished athlete, my mother could have become a poet. She still emanates—as most writers do—that simple yet complete love of words: the sight, sound, and smell of books delight her. During my childhood, she often recited favorite poems, many of which she had copied during high school into a small notebook, now yellowed with age and stacked on my own writing desk. Some days, I flip through the poems she had collected and picture her returning from a high school basketball game with friends—their voices echoing the rhythm of dribbling—to immerse herself in another mesmerizing cadence of meter. When I replay in my mind a sonnet she first intercepted, I can't help but acknowledge an assist: she's passed her love for words to me, and the layup is good. Ah, how imagination grabs sentiment and scores the split-second-before-the-buzzer, near-impossible shot!

Whatever the initial tip-off, her passion for literature was contagious. We read daily—together and alone—so that well before first grade I was a confirmed bookworm, reading in the branches of trees, upside down on couches, and, of course, late at night in bed with a flashlight. These days it seems only natural that I was then, as my students are now, inspired to further action through the motion of writing.

In this way also, my mother continued her coaching role. Several times a year, she would type my childhood poems and stories into "books," which she then displayed as proudly as any basketball trophy. Such early and frequent acknowledgments confirmed for me the importance of art. When more expertise was required, she didn't hesitate in introducing her then preteen daughter to a more advanced "coach," a female college student focusing on creative writing at Ohio State. My mother even encouraged me to compete, not in athletics but in school and church writing competitions, and thus to become part of a larger community/team of young authors. Here, again, I was following her basketball driveway lessons of personal dedication and team cooperation.

Recently, my now eighty-year-old mother reminisced about her own adolescent choices of merging teamwork and individual achievement. Even as a young, tall girl in the 1940s, it would have been natural for her to lean toward baseball; after all, she came from a baseball family. Her great uncle was the legendary Branch Rickey. At the time my mother was leading her school basketball team, Branch Rickey already was laying the groundwork for his "great social experiment"; less than a year after my mother's 1946 high school graduation, Jackie Robinson would break Major League Baseball's color barrier. Later, my mother would travel with her great uncle to games and eventually attend his beloved Ohio Wesleyan University. But as a teenage girl, she did not want a ball and bat. She wanted a hoop.

When her grandfather attached a basketball hoop to their garage, she gained both a sport she loved and a gathering place for friends. Her driveway quickly became the impromptu spot for neighborhood games. Here is a photo I would love to have: my mother caught midmotion on that driveway; one arched foot six inches off the ground; her arms stretched back and high, wrists cocked in a pass to the neighbor boy, Jack Koch, seconds before his exaggerated dunk that would make her throw back her head and laugh her rare, fall-apart laughter I love to hear.

And here's another photo I would like: my mother posed in her yearbook, neat in her royal-blue team dickie, her teammates huddled around her, the caption reading "Ann Willard tossed in 8 points against Roberta Clark's lead of 5 for the seniors" typed across the bottom. Somewhere, that snapshot lays, but not in my mother's attic, from which she uncovered the neatly packed yearbook that displayed the caption. And not in her own photo albums, which we studied once again this summer, reliving choices and experiences that made us both who we've become. But she is sure the photo exists, and, in turn, it continues as such in our memories.

What I have instead is an image I didn't expect—my sister, my mother, and myself on vacation, celebrating my fiftieth and my mother's eightieth birthday. It's late afternoon in Niagara-on-the-Lake. We're just leaving the auditorium of the crowded King Albert Theatre. The director has taken the crafted script and, through his coaching, balanced the skills of individual players with the overall talent of the ensemble. Though the beat of the standing ovation has faded, we're still caught in the motion and rhythm of the playwright's words. In our enthusiasm, we almost forget my mother's wheelchair at the back of the theater: a "temporary assist," we've assured her, just for the trip.

Out in the lobby, a friendly stranger comments on our obvious joy and offers to snap our photo. There's my sister, who reminds me that she also played high school basketball. There's my mother, who, graceful even in her wheelchair, lets loose her uninhibited laugh. And there, there, I am, who, between teaching and writing, sometimes plays H-O-R-S-E and P-I-G with my son, daughter, and husband on our suburban driveway. At that moment in that lobby, we're a team huddled together, posing for a new fan with a camera. There, in that quick flash—like a Patrick Ewing foul shot suspended in a poem—this observer captures who we are.

And then we're in motion again. I pile my arms full with our "equipment"—purses, programs, the camera. My sister grips the handles of my mother's wheelchair. My mother pushes off with her not-as-strong legs. Together, we three pivot just-so out into the afternoon light. Then we go exactly where we want to go.

SQUEAK FROM SHOES

RICHARD NEWMAN

THIS WEEKEND OUR FAMILY WILL PLAY IN FIVE BASKETBALL GAMES. I will play in two and attend my daughter's three select league games (plus her two soccer games), and her school's basketball season hasn't even started yet. One weekend we played eight games.

A few years ago I started dreaming I was playing basketball nearly every single night, waking up my then-girlfriend by diving for loose balls and banking turnaround jump shots. The strange thing about these dreams was that I had barely played basketball since eighth grade, twenty-five years before.

The dreams became so regular and the urge to play again so strong that I asked for, and received, from that same then-girlfriend, a basketball goal for Christmas. I began playing with friends and my daughter in our driveway. We waged small but epic battles between the slope to the alley and the battered wooden fence. Later my daughter's school drafted me to coach her fourth-grade basketball team. I was apparently the only parent who had ever played.

My next girlfriend had played basketball in high school and understood my fascination. On one of our first "dates" we played H-O-R-S-E, and she later admitted my shot was ugly and she let me win. I married her anyway. Before we got married, though, I asked her to help me coach the fourth-grade girls team, and that's when basketball started taking over our days and evenings as well as my dreams.

My daughter fell in love with the game, too, and the three of us went to her school's gym on nonpractice days to shoot around and work on her free throws and layups. One day a bunch of guys burst into the gym like they owned it. They had a regular Sunday afternoon pickup game and asked me to play too. Soon I was playing regularly in their Sunday and Wednesday games, comprised of teachers, doctors, stockbrokers, a house painter, a chemist, a couple lawyers, and a stained-glass window refurbisher. The principal of the school, who also played with us, approached me before a game once and said, "You play very aggressively for a poet!" and invited me to play in his Saturday morning group. That 6:30 A.M. basketball game is the only thing I've ever willingly gotten up early to do in my life. I have always been a night owl and would stay up until 4:00 A.M. every night and sleep until noon if I could. I still stay up late, hitting our local tavern, the Cat's Meow, with my wife and friends on Friday or Saturday nights, but every Saturday morning I get up, often hung over, sometimes still drunk, in the black-and-blue cold, to play basketball.

I have since invited some of my friends to these regular games, two or three poets and a fiction writer, and no one has made any more cracks about playing aggressively for a bunch of poets. Poets are as ruthless as politicians, often because they have to be politicians, but we are all passionate about the game and bring an intensity (if not always conviction) to the court three days a week. If I had the time and could find another regular game, I would probably play four days a week, though my body would rebel—more than it does now. I'm already stiff and sore, a pathetic sight to see hobbling down stairs every morning like a heavy old man, prodding myself on with a sad refrain of "Ooh!" "Aah!" "Ouch!" and choice profanity.

In addition to sore knees and ankles, my fingers are crooked from so many jams—the best is when they swell up like fat purple slugs. My back regularly hurts, especially when I sit down to write. I've had tendonitis of the shoulder for months at a time. I rarely have all my toenails on my right foot—and those existing toenails are often purple or black, hanging on by dried blood. I currently have a collection of exuberant bruises—one on my left bicep, courtesy of Michael's swipe, and one in the ribs, thanks to Len's wickedly sharp elbow.

All this begs the question: Why do we do it? I have asked myself many times, especially on Saturday mornings trying to find my gym shorts in the cold darkness after only a couple hours of drunken sleep.

The most obvious answer is a love of the game itself. I love playing full court, connecting to cutters with passes to the rim. I love the ongoing one-on-one matchups as we all strive to improve our game despite our failing, slowing bodies. I love playing defense—the challenge I usually put on myself of guarding either the biggest or fastest guy on the court.

Perhaps most of all, I love rebounding. Even more than scoring, I love the thrill of jumping through a throng of players and wrenching the ball out of the air, of getting just a fingertip above the enemy to tip the ball to myself and snag one for our team, of boxing out my guy, pulling one down and lobbing it down the court to a teammate for a layup. Going after loose balls is instinctive—even if we have too many players and it's my turn to sit out 10 points, when a loose ball bounces anywhere near me, it's all I can do not to dive onto the court. Fetch, fetch, keep fetching, boy! If I had a tail, it would wag fast enough to cool the gym.

Yes, we play for love of the game, but the best games, as well as the best writing about games, always enact something larger than the actual game. The game is not so much a metaphor but a vehicle for showing what is most essential in ourselves. It helps us enact our stories, our strengths and weaknesses, our heart and our drive, on a grander stage than the office cubicle or the backyard with the lawn mower.

In the best games, there is always something at stake. Most of us want to win or lose—and at the very least to know how we measure up. When I coached grade-school soccer, the kids in our first grade "scoreless" leagues always kept score themselves, even if the other team routed us. We want to know if we're winners or losers, in life as well as in tiddlywinks.

The main reason I think we play and watch games, however, and not just basketball, is not for something larger than the game itself but something smaller: being in or witnessing the moment of a game well played.

Nature, for example, did not give me outstanding height, grace, or even a good shot. My three-days-a-week basketball teams lose at least as many as we win, and I'm sure if anybody showed me footage of us playing I would cringe and never step onto hardwood again. But every now and then I play close to the idealized image of myself as a basketball player that I carry in my mind. Everybody in our group does. One day we can't even draw iron on a shot, can't dribble except off our feet, can't even pass to somebody on our own team. Then suddenly, the next day, if only briefly, someone will hit several threes in a row or find a magical jump-shot rhythm or make an almost acrobatic move to the rim or play unstoppable and indefatigable, total shutdown, shot-blocking defense.

As with so many other activities, not just sports or the arts but also business, science, or education, this phenomenon can only be described as inspiration. It often strikes suddenly, when it shouldn't, say when a person has a cold or is hung over or stayed up all night with a sick child. It famously fosters superstition and ritual—how many times a baseball player adjusts straps or taps his helmet before stepping up to the plate. Wade Boggs ate chicken before every baseball game and drew the Hebrew word for life in the batter's box before every at-bat, although he was not Jewish. Point guard Mike Bibby clips his nails every time he goes to the bench, starting from the first timeout. I know several writers who can only write with a certain kind of pen or with a mug of green tea in front of them.

Despite our pretense of rationality, we practice silly rituals and superstitions because this "inspiration" lies just beyond our control. Our love of "the game," and the thrill and wonder at inspired play, drives us through the drudgery of practice and the failures of missed shots, strikeouts, pop flies, bad passes, and muffed but perfectly metrical pieces of crap. Or rejections.

In writing poetry or playing basketball (or cooking or painting or anything else) the best moments occur when we receive the words or motions unconsciously, instinctively, immediately. It is a rare but wondrous experience, barely remembered afterwards or recollected through a haze. The clichés are true: time slows down. A ball seems poised in the air, and we think, "Why isn't anybody else grabbing it?" Suddenly, not even aware of what we are doing, we have snatched the ball, taken a dribble and spun to the basket for a shot—and even more miraculously, it has gone in!

The same goes for writing. Most of the poets I know tell me they write their best work quickly and unself-consciously with only minor revisions, while laboring with draft after draft over the mediocre ones. This is not to say writers shouldn't work every day and instead sit around idly waiting for a text from the muse.

Coming at it fresh can help. I often play my best basketball after a week off (sprained ankle, honeymoon). I've noticed other guys in our group do, too. But we've been playing three days a week for years and work out on off-days, so we won't collapse trying to run full court. We understand the game and have developed our own sets of skills, limited as they might be, so that if we don't think about it too much, rely on muscle memory, and let the game come to us without getting angry or forcing it, we play much better.

In writing, if technical skills and fundamentals—(use muscular verbs, listen for overmodification, avoid familiar phrases, etc.)—aren't in place, the writer will be unprepared when the wondrous and mysterious combinations of metaphor, music, and voice strike from nowhere. A lifetime of playing, reading, working, practicing, watching other games is worth those moments of pure, unconscious activity, what I think we mean when we say "poetry in motion," even if they last no longer than a phrase or fraction of a second, no longer than the squeak from shoes.

Oddly enough, I still dream about playing basketball almost as much as before. Playing three games a week and watching and sometimes coaching my daughter's two or three games a week didn't get those hoop dreams out of my system. I still wake up both myself and my wife bounding for rebounds. You can't blame a guy for his dreams, only whether he chooses to act on them or not, so I have another decision to make these days. Lately I've been dreaming a lot about playing in a rock-and-roll band again.

OVERTIME

ANNOUNCING MY RETIREMENT

J. D. SCRIMGEOUR

On New Year's Eve my family and I were in our nation's capital, in a hotel less than half a mile from the White House. It was the first time my two sons, ages thirteen and ten, had been to Washington. We had spent much of the previous week walking up and down the Mall, checking out the museums and monuments. Along some streets, wooden scaffolding and bleachers reminded us that Barack Obama was soon to be inaugurated. Obama's face was on the pins and T-shirts being sold by the outdoor vendors in the week's spring-like warmth, on the covers of newspapers and magazines in the drugstores. The enthusiasm felt real, palpable, and as I stood with my sons reading the words of Lincoln carved high into the shadows of his memorial, I couldn't help but believe that the country was experiencing a rebirth.

When I returned home to Salem, Massachusetts, I was brimming with energy, and it found its release in my enthusiasms: I spent much of the first weeks after the visit to D.C. writing poetry and playing basketball. I began a new file on my computer, "Journal 2009" and added a poem to it almost daily. And I was playing basketball at the local Y at least twice a week, regaining some form to my jumper. In some ways, I was reliving my years in graduate school in Indiana, when I had time and leisure to indulge in these twin passions. I wouldn't begin teaching until the day after the inauguration, my boys had returned to school, and so I had a few weeks that felt as wide open as a breezy Bloomington summer.

What happened, of course, is what always happens: the weight of time and the world. In other words, I had to write my department's five-year program review and read all my students' writing, and I badly sprained my wrist when I got bowled over by a guy with forty pounds on me when he drove wildly to the basket. Suddenly it didn't seem so urgent—it didn't even seem possible—to type up a poem in the morning, or to battle twenty-somethings for rebounds.

Now, the semester is over, Barack Obama has just made a speech in Cairo about the nation's relation to the Muslim world, and I'm beginning to write poems again. I haven't returned to the gym.

When I was in Indiana, I was part of a group of English graduate students who played basketball every Saturday morning. Some winters, one of us would take the initiative to sign us up for the graduate school's intramural league. Playing against competitive future lawyers, doctors, and MBAs, we usually managed, somehow, to hold our own. One close game we won in overtime against a team from the law school, and as we walked past them after it was over, I heard their coach (they were competitive enough to have a coach) berate their players: "You know who you guys just lost to?" he snarled, "You just lost to a bunch of poets!"

Perhaps I should have stopped playing ball right then. It would have been a memorable exit.

Certainly, one of the joys of basketball is proving yourself in a forum in which the final score is the undebatable arbiter. For poets, publication and recognition can seem as much about who you know as what you write, but there is no doubt about whether you hit that game-winning fadeaway to win the rubber game at the Y. Obama, our first president who takes hoops seriously, was attracted to the game in part by this quality. He writes in his memoir that while in high school he would play on the University of

Hawaii courts, "where a handful of black men, mostly gym rats and has-beens, would teach me an attitude that didn't just have to do with the sport. That respect came from what you did and not who your daddy was." The poets could beat the lawyers!

So, basketball could be about earned respect. Poetry can be, too, when it is read aloud. At a reading, a poet's honors and prizes rarely disguise weak work. There needs to be a connection with the audience, just as, in basketball, there needs to be a connection between the players. Obama knew about this sense of connection, too, that there was "something nobody talked about: a way of being together when the game was tight and the sweat broke and the best players stopped worrying about their points and the worst players got swept up in the moment and the score only mattered because that's how you sustained the trance. In the middle of which you might make a move or a pass that surprised even you, so that even the guy guarding you had to smile, as if to say, 'Damn . . .'"

The unspoken sense of "being together" in a "trance." While the dynamics are different, this seems similar to what can happen at a poetry reading, when the poet isn't trotting out his latest villanelle to impress, but exposing what is human—when the students required to attend shut their cell phones and stop texting and become aware of the words filling the air, present as a body. And they become aware of the actual bodies around them, the crossed legs in jeans of the person beside them, the small mole on the back of the neck of the man in front of them. The world bristles with clarity.

One Christmas when I was a teenager, my uncle John and aunt Kathie gave me Bill Russell's autobiography, *Second Wind: The Memoirs of an Opinionated Man.* I was just starting to get hooked on basketball, staying after school every day to play in the upstairs gym at the high school and occasionally breaking a finger. I recall waiting in pain in the school lobby for a ride to the hospital, showing some girls my ring finger, bent backward toward my face, and listening to them squeal in horror.

Russell's book taught me a lot about race, and competing, but the passages that I'll never forget were about how Russell really began to learn basketball. By his account, he was a mediocre player in high school, but his height landed him on a traveling all-star team. When he rode the bench for that team, Russell marveled at the star player, Bill Treu. Always cerebral, Russell studied Treu's moves, and began trying a few himself, if only in his mind, inserting himself into Treu's place. But Russell wasn't the size of Treu, and he couldn't make many of the moves that he studied, so, he writes, "more or less as a lark, I started imagining myself in plays *with* Treu. He'd be spinning in for a layup, and I'd be shadowing him on defense. Since I knew his moves so well, I'd imagine myself as his mirror image. I'd take a step backward for every step he took forward, and so forth. It was as if we were dancing, with Treu leading. When I saw him go up to lay the ball in the basket, I'd see myself go up and block the shot. I enjoyed the two-man show in my mind, so I expanded it. I sketched out scenes of Treu and me fast breaking together, pirouetting together, hanging in the air together. Any way he bent, I'd bend with him."

This isn't everybody's basketball, but it became mine. Although I was quick and agile enough to squirm to the hoop for layups or get some fast-break points, I became someone who studied the opposition, who recognized that there were only so many ways to put the ball into the basket, and I just had to discover how my opponent liked to do it, then stop that. Basketball became a dance, and it was one that I was making up. For Russell, the first time he actually used one of his moves on Treu in practice, he was "ecstatic." It wasn't because he had become as good as Treu. He hadn't. But it was because the moves were the first that he "had invented. . . . They grew out of my imagination, and so I saw them as my own." Like Russell, the thrill of inventing, of making something with my body, drew me in.

When I first came to poetry, the thrill of making was similar. I recall nights late in my college dorm room, scratching out words in my notebook rather than doing homework, counting the syllables in each line. Like Russell, I may have even closed my eyes as I tested different phrases. I wasn't trying to match any set form or meter. Even then, early on, I knew my allegiances were with free verse. I wanted to discover my own patterns, my own moves.

After his passages about what basketball meant to him as a youth, Obama writes, "My wife will roll her eyes right about now." Her scorn is because—there's no denying it—basketball is a young man's game, and there seems something foolish about middle-aged men getting reverential about it. The joy of basketball is a youthful joy, a joy of the body. When I have basketball dreams, they are never about me being more clever than I am on the court, they are about me—all 5'7" of me—being able to soar and dunk. I love those rare dreams, but, of course, they are goofy. They are.

For me, basketball does not mean what it once did. Not only does it have different appeal, it has, frankly, less appeal. I will watch some of the NCAA basketball tournament or the NBA playoffs on television, but almost always, as I'm watching, I am aware that I could be doing something else, like writing. The games seem to have taken on a kind of sameness that is dull. I'm sure they were always like this; I know that one of the joys of watching Bernard King, my favorite player when I was in college, was the way he was mechanically good. He'd make the same shot, over and over—that turnaround from the baseline. So it's probably changes in me, not changes in the game. The thrill and fascination for the sport that I used to have I see now in my boys, who obsess over March Madness. I smile remembering that one of their favorite D.C. memories was the night that they played pop-a-shot for hours at the ESPN Zone.

When I was thirty-five, I decided to take a modern dance class at the college where I teach. At the end of the semester, we all had to compose a piece of choreography and present it to the class. Most students put together a minute of simple dance moves to some pop song. I recorded my voice reading a lyric paragraph from an essay that I had written about basketball, and came up with some moves to accompany the rhythm of the words. I practiced it in my tiny living room, and when the day came to present, I wowed the class, spinning and gliding across the hardwood dance floor. I incorporated one or two moves from basketball, but mostly the movement was abstract—it wasn't too corny. That class might have been my first real step away from basketball. I had once turned to basketball so I could dance, and now I was turning to dance so I could ball.

As I have gotten older—and I'm forty-four, not sixty-four—I've come to rely more and more on my bag of tricks on the court, what I've learned from years playing the game: how to fool an opponent by pretending I'm not paying attention, then stepping into a passing lane, or, on offense, zipping a pass by some young guy's head for a layup when he turns his back to the ball. While these moments are satisfying, they aren't about the thrill of discovery, the joy of dance. They are about showing others what they don't know, sensing weakness and exploiting it.

Writing this essay, I've realized that I might not ever need to play basketball again. I recall when I tore my ACL, a common basketball injury, when I was thirty. When I told my wife that it was unclear when and how I would be able to play again, I started to cry. Now, thinking about never rushing down the court to fill a lane, or never picking some young guy's pocket when he gets too cocky, doesn't fill me with sadness. In fact, typing that last line, I could feel my body letting out a little "Hip, hip hooray!" I'll probably go out into our dusty backyard and play against my boys until they both are good enough to beat me, and then I'll hang up the hightops for good. Poetry is how I dance now.

TEAM ROSTER

COACH

TODD DAVIS IS THE AUTHOR OF FOUR BOOKS OF POEMS—*THE LEAST of These* (2010), *Household of Water, Moon, and Snow: The Thoreau Poems* (2010), *Some Heaven* (2007), and *Ripe* (2002)—and coeditor of *Making Poems: 40 Poems with Commentary by the Poets* (2010). His poetry has been featured on the radio by Garrison Keillor, on *The Writer's Almanac*, and by Marion Roach on *The Naturalist's Datebook*, as well as by Ted Kooser in his syndicated newspaper column *American Life in Poetry*. His poems have won the Gwendolyn Brooks Poetry Prize, have been nominated for the Pushcart Prize, and have appeared in such journals and magazines as *Poetry Daily, Verse Daily, Iowa Review, North American Review, Indiana Review, Gettysburg Review, Shenandoah, West Branch, River Styx, Arts & Letters, Quarterly West, Green Mountains Review, Nimrod, Sou'wester,* and *Poetry East*. He teaches creative writing and environmental studies at Penn State University's Altoona College.

PLAYERS

Therese Becker's poetry, essays, journalism, and photography have been widely published in various literary journals, newspapers, magazines and anthologies, including *Poetry East, Beloit Poetry Journal, DoubleTake, New York Quarterly, Puerto del Sol, Witness, Contemporary Michigan Poetry: Poems from the Third Coast,* and *The Anthology of Magazine Verse.* A chapbook of her poetry and photography, *The Fear of Cameras,* was published by Ridgeway Press.

Patricia Clark is Poet-in-Residence and Professor in the Department of Writing at Grand Valley State University. She is the author of three books of poetry: *She Walks into the Sea* (2009), *My Father on a Bicycle* (2005), and *North of Wondering* (1999). Her poetry has appeared in magazines such as *Atlantic Monthly, Slate, Poetry, Mississippi Review, Gettysburg Review, New England Review, Northwest Review,* and *North American Review.* She has also coedited an anthology of contemporary women writers called *Worlds in Our Words.* Her chapbook of poems, *Given the Trees,* is one of the initial four in a series from the American Land Publishing Project. Clark's work has been featured on *Poetry Daily* and *Verse Daily;* she has won the Gwendolyn Brooks Prize twice, *Mississippi Review*'s Poetry Prize; and has been honored as Second Prize winner in the 2005 Pablo Neruda / Nimrod International Journal Poetry competition. The recipient of an Artist Grant from ArtServe Michigan, Clark was invited with two other poets to open the Library of Congress's noon reading series in Washington, D.C., in fall 2005. Clark served as Poet Laureate of Grand Rapids, Michigan, from 2005 to 2007.

Jim Daniels is the winner of the Blue Lynx Poetry Prize for his book *Revolt of the Crash Test Dummies* (2007). Two other books were published in 2007, his third collection of short fiction, *Mr. Pleasant,* and his eleventh book of poems, *In Line for the Exterminator.* In 2005, Daniels wrote and produced the independent film, *Dumpster,* which appeared in more than a dozen film festivals, and published *Street,* a book of poems accompanying the photographs of Charlee Brodsky. His most recent book of poems is *Having a Little Talk with Capital P Poetry* (2011). He is the winner of the Tillie Olsen Prize, the Brittingham Prize for Poetry, two fellowships from the National Endowment for the Arts, and two fellowships from the Pennsylvania Council on the Arts. His poems have appeared in the Pushcart Prize and *Best American Poetry* anthologies. He is the Thomas Stockman Baker Professor of English at Carnegie Mellon University, where he directs the Creative Writing Program.

Natalie Diaz was born and raised in the Fort Mojave Indian Village in Needles, California. She is Mojave and Pima. She was a member of the 1997 NCAA Division I Finalist women's basketball team at Old Dominion University. After playing professional basketball in Europe and Asia, she returned to Old Dominion where she completed her MFA in 2007. She has poetry and fiction published in the *Iowa Review, Nimrod, Crab Orchard Review, Prairie Schooner, North American Review, Narrative,* and others. She lives in Surprise, Arizona, where she teaches, sells snow cones, and conducts plyometric and agility training camps.

Stephen Dunn is the author of fifteen books of poetry and two of prose. His *Different Hours* was awarded the Pulitzer Prize in 2001, and his two most recent books are *What Goes On: Selected & New Poems 1995–2009* and *Here and Now: Poems,* both from Norton. His awards included the Academy Award in Literature from the American Academy of Arts & Letters, fellowships from the Guggenheim and Rockefeller foundations, and the Paterson Award for Sustained Literary Achievement. He is Distinguished Professor of Creative Writing at Richard Stockton College of New Jersey, and lives in Frostburg, Maryland.

Gary Fincke is the Charles B. Degenstein Professor of English and Creative Writing at Susquehanna University. Winner of the Flannery O'Connor Award for Short Fiction and the Ohio State University / The Journal Poetry Prize, he has published twenty-two books of poetry, short fiction, and nonfiction, most recently the memoir *The Canals of Mars* (2010), *The*

Fire Landscape: Poems (2008), *Standing around the Heart: Poems* (2005), *Sorry I Worried You* (2004), and *Amp'd: A Father's Backstage Pass*, a non-fiction account of his son's life as a rock guitarist in the band Breaking Benjamin (2004). Winner of the Bess Hokin Prize from *Poetry* magazine and the Rose Lefcowitz Prize from *Poet Lore*, Fincke has received a PEN Syndicated Fiction Prize as well as seven fellowships for creative writing from the Pennsylvania Council on the Arts. His poems, stories, and essays have appeared in such periodicals as *Harper's, Newsday, Paris Review, Kenyon Review, Georgia Review, American Scholar,* and *DoubleTake.* He has twice been awarded Pushcart Prizes for his work, been recognized by *Best American Stories,* and been cited nine times in the past eleven years for a "Notable Essay" in *Best American Essays.* His essay "The Canals of Mars" was reprinted in *The Pushcart Essays,* an anthology of the best nonfiction printed during the first twenty-five years of the Pushcart Prize volumes.

Linda Nemec Foster is the author of nine collections of poetry including *Amber Necklace from Gdansk* (a finalist for the Ohio Book Award in Poetry) and *Listen to the Landscape* (short-listed for the Michigan Notable Book Award). Her most recent book, *Talking Diamonds,* was published in 2009 by New Issues Press. Foster's poems have appeared in such journals as *Georgia Review, New American Writing, North American Review, Nimrod,* and *Aethlon: The Journal of Sports Literature.* She has received awards for her work from ArtServe Michigan, the Michigan Foundation for the Arts, the National Writers' Voice, and the Academy of American Poets. She founded the Contemporary Writers Series at Aquinas College and currently is a member of the Series' programming committee.

Ross Gay is the author of two poetry collections, *Bringing the Shovel Down* (2011) and *Against Which* (2006). His poems have appeared in *American Poetry Review, Atlanta Review, Harvard Review, Columbia: A Journal of Poetry and Art,* and *Margie: The American Journal of Poetry,* among other places. He teaches at Indiana University and in the low-residency program at New England College. He is a Cave Canem fellow.

214

Margaret Gibson is the author of the memoir *The Prodigal Daughter: Reclaiming an Unfinished Childhood* (2008), and of ten books of poetry: *Second Nature* (2010); *One Body* (2007); *Autumn Grasses* (2003); *Icon and Evidence* (2001); *Earth Elegy: New and Selected Poems* (1997); *The Vigil, A Poem in Four Voices*, a Finalist for the National Book Award in 1993; *Out in the Open* (1989); *Memories of the Future: The Daybooks of Tina Modotti*, cowinner of the Melville Dane Award of the Poetry Society of America in 1986–87; *Long Walks in the Afternoon*, the 1982 Lamont Selection of the Academy of American Poets; and *Signs* (1979). Gibson has been a Visiting Professor at the University of Connecticut since 1993. She has been awarded a National Endowment for the Arts Grant, a Lila Wallace / Reader's Digest Fellowship, and grants from the Connecticut Commission on the Arts. "Earth Elegy," the title poem of *New and Selected Poems*, won the James Boatwright III Prize for Poetry. "Archaeology" was awarded a Pushcart Prize in 2001.

Jeff Gundy's five books of poems include, most recently, *Spoken among the Trees* (2007), winner of the Poetry Award from the Society of Midland Authors, and *Deerflies* (2004), winner of the Editions Poetry Prize and the Nancy Dasher Award. His prose books include *Walker in the Fog: On Mennonite Writing* (2005), chosen for the Dale W. Brown Book Award, *Scattering Point: The World in a Mennonite Eye* (2003), and *A Community of Memory: My Days with George and Clara* (1996). He was a Fulbright Lecturer at the University of Salzburg in Austria in 2008. Other awards include multiple fellowships from the Ohio Arts Council, two C. Henry Smith Peace Lectureships, numerous Pushcart Prize nominations, and a share of a Silver Gamma Award for reviewing. A regular reviewer of poetry and nonfiction for the *Georgia Review*, he also served as General Editor of the Intro Journals Project of the Association of Writers and Writing Programs, and has served on the faculty of the Antioch Writers Workshop. He helped to found the Language of Nature conference, bringing together writers and naturalists, at Cuyahoga Valley National Park. His poems and essays have appeared in *Kenyon Review, Cincinnati Review, Georgia Review, Antioch Review, Image, The Sun, Colorado Review, Creative Nonfiction, Quarterly West, River Styx, Tampa*

Review, *Witness*, *Poetry Northwest*, *Pleiades*, and many other magazines. He teaches writing, literature, and other courses at Bluffton University in Ohio.

Marian Haddad, poet and writer, is based in San Antonio, Texas, and works as a manuscript and publishing consultant, visiting writer, public speaker, and arts-event coordinator. Her work is published in numerous literary journals and anthologies in the United States, Brussels, the United Kingdom, and the Middle East. Her chapbook *Saturn Falling Down* was published in 2003 at the request of Texas Public Radio in correlation with their Hands-On Poetry Workshops. Her full-length collection of poems, *Somewhere between Mexico and a River Called Home* (2004) was recommended by *Valparaiso Poetry Review* and noted by *Small Press Review* upon its publication. She has taught creative writing at Our Lady of the Lake University and Northwest Vista College, and American and International Literature at St. Mary's University.

William Heyen was born in Brooklyn, New York, in 1940. He is Professor of English and Poet-in-Residence Emeritus at SUNY Brockport. He has received Fulbright, Guggenheim, NEA, American Academy and Institute of Arts and Letters, and other awards. Among his books, *Noise in the Trees* (1974) was an American Library Association "Notable Book"; *Crazy Horse in Stillness* (1996) won the Small Press Book Award for Poetry in 1997; and *Shoah Train: Poems* (2004) was a finalist for the National Book Award. His manuscripts and correspondence are archived at Ohio University, the University of Rochester, and at the Beinecke Library of Yale University. Perhaps the most prolific American poet of his generation, his work has also appeared in several hundred anthologies and in periodicals such as the *New Yorker*, *Harper's*, *Atlantic Monthly*, *American Poetry Review*, *Southern Review*, and *Poetry*.

Lauren (Jentz) Jensen grew up in northern Michigan, where her love for basketball began with a crush on Bryan Southerton in the seventh grade and a desire to impress him on the court. Although she never landed a date, Lauren continued to play basketball and eventually took her game to Hope College. It was here, in her coach's office, where she read a poem by the poet

Jack Ridl pinned to the wall, signed up for a workshop, and began writing. In 2004 she moved to Oregon, where she spent the following years working in a woodshop, coaching, traveling, and writing her way to the East Coast. She is a recent MFA graduate of Virginia Tech University, and now lives in Eugene, Oregon, where she serves as cofounder and Assistant Editor of *Toad,* an online journal.

Mary Linton is a wetland ecologist and aquatic biologist whose poems have appeared in *Appalachia, Aethlon: The Journal of Sport Literature, Blueline, Builder, Country Feedback, Poetry Motel, Seeding the Snow,* and the anthology *Making Poems: 40 Poems with Commentary by the Poets* (2010). Her ecological articles have appeared in *Evolution, Ecology, Evolutionary Ecology, Canadian Entomology, Herpetological Review, American Naturalist,* and the *Proceedings of the Indiana Academy of Sciences,* as well as popular magazines.

Marjorie Maddox has published *Perpendicular As I* (1994 Sandstone Book Award); *Transplant, Transport, Transubstantiation* (2004); *Weeknights at the Cathedral* (Yellowglen Prize, 2006); *When the Wood Clacks Out Your Name: Baseball Poems* (2001 Redgreene Press Award); six chapbooks, and over 350 poems, stories, and essays in such journals and anthologies as *Poetry, Prairie Schooner, Crab Orchard Review, American Literary Review, Seattle Review,* and *Anthology of Magazine Verse and Yearbook of American Poetry.* She is the coeditor of *Common Wealth: Contemporary Poets on Pennsylvania* (2005) and author of two children's books: *A Crossing of Zebras: Animal Packs in Poetry* (2008) and *The Rules of the Game: Baseball Poems* (2009). The recipient of *Seattle Review's* Bentley Prize for Poetry, an Academy of American Poets Award, Cornell University's Chasen Award, and the Paumanok Poetry Award, Maddox lives with her husband and two children in Williamsport, Pennsylvania, and is Director of Creative Writing and Professor of English at Lock Haven University.

Debra Marquart is Professor of English in the MFA Program in Creative Writing & Environment at Iowa State University. Her books include two poetry collections—*Everything's a Verb* and *From Sweetness*—and a short story collection, *The Hunger Bone: Rock & Roll Stories*, which draws on her experiences as a road musician. Her work has appeared in numerous journals including *North American Review, Three Penny Review, New Letters, River City, Crab Orchard Review, Cumberland Poetry Review, Sun Magazine, Southern Poetry Review*, and *Witness*. Marquart's memoir, *The Horizontal World: Growing Up Wild in the Middle of Nowhere*, was a 2008 Booksense Pick and was awarded the 2007 PEN USA Creative Nonfiction Award. She is a recipient of a Pushcart Prize, the Shelby Foote Nonfiction Prize from the Faulkner Society, the Elle Lettres Award from *Elle* magazine, and a National Endowment for the Arts Prose Fellowship.

Adrian Matejka's first collection of poems, *The Devil's Garden*, won the 2002 Kinereth Gensler Award from Alice James Books. His second collection, *Mixology*, was a winner of the 2008 National Poetry Series. He is the recipient of awards from the Illinois Arts Council, and his work has appeared in *American Poetry Review, Gulf Coast, Pleiades, Prairie Schooner*, and *St. Louis Post-Dispatch* among other periodicals and anthologies. He teaches at Southern Illinois University Edwardsville, where he also serves as Poetry Editor for the literary journal *Sou'wester*.

David McKain is the author of three books of poetry: *In Touch* (1975), *The Common Life* (1982), and *Spirit Bodies* (1990). In addition to his work in poems, McKain's autobiography, *Spellbound: Growing Up in God's Country* (1988), won the AWP Award for Non-fiction and was nominated for the Pulitzer Prize.

James McKean writes nonfiction and poetry. His poems have appeared in journals such as *Poetry, Atlantic Monthly, Georgia Review, Southern Review*, and *Poetry Northwest* among many others, and have been featured twice in Ted Kooser's *American Life in Poetry*. His nonfiction has appeared in *Crab Orchard Review, Gray's Sporting Journal, Gettysburg Review*, and *Iowa Review*, and his essays have been reprinted in *Best American Sports Writing 2003* and the *2006 Pushcart Prize* anthology. He has published two books of poems, *Headlong* (1987) and *Tree of Heaven* (1995) and a book of essays, *Home*

Stand: Growing Up in Sports (2005). *Headlong* won a Great Lakes Colleges Association's New Writer Award in Poetry, and *Tree of Heaven* won an Iowa Poetry Prize. *Home Stand* was a finalist in the nonfiction category in the 2006 Washington State Book Awards. As an undergraduate he attended Washington State University on a basketball scholarship and played from 1964 to 1968, earning first team All-Conference (PAC-8) honors his junior and senior years. He attended the Iowa Writers' Workshop (MFA in poetry, 1981) and Iowa's English Department (PhD in American Literature and poetry writing, 1990). A Professor Emeritus at Mount Mercy College in Cedar Rapids, Iowa, he still teaches for the Queens University low-residency MFA program in Charlotte, North Carolina, at the Tinker Mountain Writers Workshop at Hollins University in Roanoke, Virginia, and for the Iowa Summer Writing Festival in Iowa City, Iowa.

Richard Newman is the author of two full-length poetry collections: *Domestic Fugues* (2009) and *Borrowed Towns* (2005). He is also the author of several poetry chapbooks, including *24 Tall Boys: Dark Verse for Light Times* (2008) and *Monster Gallery: 19 Terrifying and Amazing Monster Sonnets!* (2005). His poems have recently appeared in *Best American Poetry*, *Boulevard*, *Crab Orchard Review*, *New Letters*, *Pleiades*, *Poetry East*, *Tar River Poetry*, *Seriously Funny: Poems about Love, God, War, Art, Sex, Madness, and Everything Else* (2009), *The Sun*, and many other periodicals and anthologies. His poems have also been featured in Ted Kooser's *American Life in Poetry*, Garrison Keillor's *Writer's Almanac*, *Poetry Daily*, and *Verse Daily*. For the last fifteen years he has served as editor of *River Styx* and codirector of the River Styx at Duff's reading series.

Jack Ridl's latest collection is *Losing Season* from CavanKerry Press. The book explores life during a long, hard winter in a small town that is obsessed with its high school basketball team's losing season. Ridl's previous full collection, *Broken Symmetry*, was corecipient of the Society of Midland Authors award for best book of poetry published in 2006. His *Against Elegies* was chosen by former U.S. poet laureate Billy Collins for the Center for Book Arts (NYC) Chapbook Award. He is also author of the chapbook *Outside*

the Center Ring, a collection of poems based on his childhood experience
with the circus. He is also coauthor with Peter Schakel of *Approaching Literature* and of *Approaching Poetry*, both from Bedford / St. Martin's Press. In
2008, he was named by the Institute for International Sport as one of the
100 most influential people in sports. In 1996, he was named by the Carnegie Foundation as Michigan Professor of the Year. Ridl has given readings
throughout the country including being invited to the Geraldine R. Dodge
Festival. He was the keynote reader in 2010 at Springfield College in celebration of James Naismith's creating the game of basketball at the college.

Bobby C. Rogers grew up in McKenzie, Tennessee, and was educated at
Union University, the University of Tennessee at Knoxville, and the Uni-
versity of Virginia, where he held a Henry Hoyns Fellowship in Creative
Writing and studied with Charles Wright, Greg Orr, George Garrett, and
John Casey. His book *Paper Anniversary* won the 2009 Agnes Lynch Star-
rett Poetry Prize at University of Pittsburgh Press. His poetry has appeared
in *Southern Review, Georgia Review, Shenandoah, Greensboro Review, Image,
Epoch, Puerto del Sol, Iron Horse Literary Review, Southwest Review, Sou'wester,
Nimrod, Cimarron Review, Southern Humanities Review, Agni Online, Washington Square, Meridian*, and many other magazines. He has been twice
nominated for a Pushcart Prize, and he won the *Greensboro Review* Literary
Prize in Poetry for 2002. Another sporting essay entitled "Hunting Close:
On Bird Dogs and Lost Time" appeared in *Afield: Writers on Bird Dogs*,
edited by Bob DeMott and Dave Smith. Currently, he is Professor of English and Writer-in-Residence at Union University in Jackson, Tennessee. He
lives in Memphis with his wife and son and daughter.

Patrick Rosal is the author of two full-length poetry collections, *Uprock
Headspin Scramble and Dive*, which won the Members' Choice Award from
the Asian-American Writers' Workshop, and more recently *My American
Kundiman*, which won the Association of Asian American Studies 2006 Book
Award in Poetry and the Global Filipino Literary Award. He garnered a Fulbright grant as a senior U.S. Scholar to the Philippines in 2009. His poems
have been honored with the Palanquin Poetry Prize, the *Arts and Letters* Prize,

the Allen Ginsberg Award, and the James Hearst Prize. His work has been published widely in journals and anthologies, including *American Poetry Review, Harvard Review, Literary Review, Brevity: A Journal of Concise Literary Nonfiction, The Beacon Best*, and *Language for a New Century.*

J. D. Scrimgeour is the author of a book of poems, *The Last Miles* (2005), and two essay collections, *Spin Moves* (2000) and *Themes for English B* (2006), which won the Associated Writing Programs' Award for Nonfiction. His poems have won awards from the National Society of Arts & Letters, the Academy of American Poets, and the Massachusetts Cultural Council, and they have appeared in such journals and magazines as *Colorado Review, Green Mountains Review, Phoebe, Mid-American Review, Ploughshares, Poetry*, and *Tar River Poetry.* His essays have appeared in such publications as *Creative Nonfiction, Boston Globe Magazine*, and *Chronicle of Higher Education.* He coordinates the creative writing program at Salem State College.

Peter Sears won the 1999 Peregrine Smith Poetry Competition with *The Brink*, which was published by Gibbs-Smith Publisher. The book then won the 2000 Western States Book Award in Poetry and in 2009 was named one of Oregon's best books by the Oregon State Library. His poems have appeared in national magazines and newspapers such as the *New York Times, Atlantic Monthly, Rolling Stone, Orion, Christian Science Monitor, Mademoiselle, The Oregonian*, and *Mother Jones*, and in literary journals such as *Field, Antioch Review, Poetry Northwest, Iowa Review, Zyssyva, Black Warrior Review, Cimarron Review, Beloit Poetry Journal, New Letters, Ploughshares*, and *Seneca Review.* His first collection of poems, *Tour*, was published by Breitenbush Books, and he has written two supplementary teaching texts, *Secret Writing* from Teachers & Writers Collaborative and *Gonna Bake Me a Poem* from Scholastic. His fifth chapbook, *Luge*, was released in 2008. His most recent book of poems is *Green Diver* (2009). He is presently on the faculty of the Pacific University MFA Writing Program in Forest Grove, Oregon. Sears is a graduate of Yale University and the Iowa Writers Workshop. He lives in Corvallis, Oregon.

Quincy Troupe is the author of seventeen books, including eight volumes of poetry, the latest of which is *The Architecture of Language*, recipient of the 2007 Paterson Award for Sustained Literary Achievement. He received the 2003 Milt Kessler Poetry Award for *Transcircularities: New and Selected Poems* (2002), selected by *Publishers Weekly* as one of the ten best books of poetry published in 2002. He is Professor Emeritus of Creative Writing and American and Caribbean Literature at the University of California, San Diego, was the first official Poet Laureate of the State of California, and is currently editor of *Black Renaissance Noire* (soon to be renamed *Baobab*), an academic, cultural, political, and literary journal published by the Africana Studies Program and the Institute of African American Affairs at New York University. Troupe has published his poetry, articles, and essays in over 200 publications worldwide. His poetry and prose have been translated into Arabic, Spanish, French, German, Italian, Swedish, Japanese, Chinese, Danish, Portuguese, Czech, Russian, Polish, and Dutch, and he has read his work throughout the United States, Europe, Africa, Canada, the Caribbean, Columbia, Ecuador, Nicaragua, Cuba, Mexico, and Brazil. He has taught at the College of Staten Island (CUNY), University of Ghana, Legon, Lagos University, Lagos, Nigeria, and in the Columbia University Graduate Writing Program. He is the recipient of two American Book Awards: in 1980 for his poetry collection *Snake-Back Solos* (1980) and in 1990 for his nonfiction book, *Miles: The Autobiography* (1989). In 1991 Troupe received the prestigious Peabody Award for coproducing and writing the radio series *The Miles Davis Radio Project*, which aired on National Public Radio in 1990. He is two-time winner of the Heavyweight-Champion of Poetry (1994 and 1995), sponsored by the World Poetry Bout of Taos, New Mexico, and he has been a featured poet on two PBS television series on poetry: *The United States of Poetry* (1996), and Bill Moyers's *The Power of the Word* (1989), for which his segment, "The Living Language," received a 1990 Emmy Award for Television Excellence. Currently, he is writing a novel, *The Legacy of Charlie Footman* and an auto-memoir, *The Accordion Years: 1965 to 2005;* and has recorded twenty-four tracks of his poetry accompanied by musicians and produced by the Apache guitarist Bugs Salcido. The recording, as yet unnamed, is scheduled for release sometime in 2011. Troupe lives between New York City and Goyave, Guadeloupe, with his wife, Margaret.

ACKNOWLEDGMENTS

Natalie Diaz, "Two Things You Need Balls to Do: A Miscellany from a Former Professional Basketball Player Turned Poet," first appeared in the *Southeast Review* 26.1 (2007). Reprinted by permission of the author.

Stephen Dunn, "Basketball and Poetry: The Two Richies," from *Walking Light: Essays and Memoirs*. Copyright © 2001 by Stephen Dunn. Reprinted with the permission of BOA Editions, Ltd., www.boaeditions.org, and the author.

Margaret Gibson, "Notes in the Margin" first appeared in *One Body*. Reprinted by permission of Louisiana State University Press and the author.

Jeff Gundy, "Competition and Fatigue, or Basketball," first appeared in *Flatlands*. Reprinted by permission of Cleveland State University Poetry Center and the author.

William Heyen, "In the Country of Michelangelo" first appeared in *The Confessions of Doc Williams & Other Poems*. Reprinted by permission of Etruscan Press and the author.

Adrian Matejka, "Off the Rim" first appeared in *Callaloo* 28.3 (2005). Reprinted by permission of the author.

A portion of David McKain's "Basketball and Poetry: Strange Bedfellows" first appeared in *Spellbound: Growing Up in God's Country* (University of Georgia Press, 1988). Copyright © 1988 by David McKain. Reprinted by permission of the University of Georgia Press and the author.

Thanks to the following people for their encouragement and advice in the making of this book: Martha Bates, Brian Black, Joyce and Harold Davis, Shelly Davis, Chris Dombrowski, Don Flenar, Don and Punky Fox, William Heyen, Don and Melinda Lanham, Virginia Kasamis, Mary Linton, Dinty Moore, Jack Ridl, Dave Shumate, Jack Troy, and Ken Womack.

A final thanks to all of the coaches I played for and to all the ballers I've played with for the past four decades.

The editing of this book was helped by generous grants from Pennsylvania State University.